W9-BVB-413

Amazing Place

Amazing Place

What North Carolina Means to Writers

EDITED BY

MARIANNE GINGHER

The University of North Carolina Press CHAPEL HILL

Discard
NHCPL

NEW HANOVER COUNTY
PUBLIC LIBRARY
201 CHESTNUT STREET
WILMINGTON, NC 28401

This book was published with the assistance of the
Blythe Family Fund
of the University of North Carolina Press.

© 2015 The University of North Carolina Press
All rights reserved
Designed by Kimberly Bryant and set in Miller by Rebecca Evans
Manufactured in the United States of America
The paper in this book meets the guidelines for permanence and durability
of the Committee on Production Guidelines for Book Longevity of the
Council on Library Resources. The University of North Carolina Press has
been a member of the Green Press Initiative since 2003.

Cover and interior illustrations by Alyssa D'Avanzo

Library of Congress Cataloging-in-Publication Data
Amazing place : what North Carolina means to writers / edited by
Marianne Gingher.
pages cm
ISBN 978-1-4696-2239-2 (pbk : alk. paper)
ISBN 978-1-4696-2240-8 (ebook)
1. Authors, American—Homes and haunts—North Carolina.
2. Place (Philosophy) in literature. 3. North Carolina—In literature.
I. Gingher, Marianne, editor.
PS266.N8A43 2015   810.9'9756—dc23
2014026607

MIX
Paper from
responsible sources
FSC
www.fsc.org
FSC® C013483

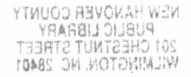

NEW HANOVER COUNTY
PUBLIC LIBRARY
201 CHESTNUT STREET
WILMINGTON, NC 28401

For my sons,

RODERICK AND SAM,

and for my brothers,

MARK, DAVID, AND JOHN,

mostly North Carolinians by birth,

and all, by heart

Contents

Down East and the Coast

Acknowledgments

This book was actually the brainchild of Zach Read, a former editor at UNC Press, and I am grateful to him for his early enthusiasm and persistence in seeing the project launched. I hope he'll be pleased with the end result. A plenitude of gratitude goes to my editor, Mark Simpson-Vos, whose patient steerage, sharp insights, and suggestions improved the manuscript in every way; to Lucas Church, Mark's assistant, for keeping me on task with the nit-picky stuff; and to Jay Mazzocchi for meticulous, eagle-eyed copyediting. Thanks to everyone at the press for making my job easier and for supporting the publication of this wonderful and unique little book. And now . . . a drumroll, if you please, because *Amazing Place* is a "first" for UNC Press: an anthology of never-before-published personal narratives by contemporary fiction and imaginative nonfiction writers. It will assume its proper niche on the shelf beside anthologies of contemporary poetry and fiction that the press has published in the past. Kudos to UNC Press for its vision.

Thanks to all the great people I work with at UNC–Chapel Hill, most importantly to my colleagues in the Department of English and Comparative Literature and in the Creative Writing Program. Special thanks to Anita Braxton, Susan Irons, Bland Simpson, Beverly Taylor, and Daniel Wallace for always having my back, and to my new colleague, Stephanie Elizondo Griest, who so gamely undertook the assignment to write a piece for this book even though she'd only been a North Carolinian for about five minutes. Gratitude to Lee Smith, too, for going the extra mile—always.

I am indebted to the Bowman and Gordon Gray Professorship Program for the grant I received that enabled me to spend time collecting and assembling the contents of this book.

Last, but by no means least, mighty thanks and thunderous cheers to the writers who signed on and delivered such, well ... *amazing* narratives. Their generosity of time and spirit, their enthusiasm, and their writing means the world to me.

Acknowledgments

Introduction

"Place" is where "we put our roots, wherever birth, chance, fate, or our traveling shoes set us down," Eudora Welty wrote. I've lived in North Carolina since I was three years old. My father was born and raised here, as were his Scottish forebears. I was educated here, and I continue to work here. My writing life began here, and I am fairly certain it will end here. I would be hard-pressed to deny that living in North Carolina has shaped me as a writer. The essence of "place" is family, friends, community, heritage, culture, weather, and landscape in all its sensory glory (or squalor), steeping in a particular containment of time. Any writer you ask will tell you that place insists upon particulars: politics, religion, race, economy, manners, jokes, fashion, music, recipes, wood smoke, the taste of sea salt, an unpaved road, a wrecking ball, a church, a swamp, an alleyway, a tobacco field, the syrupy warble of a wren, the sound of somebody humming while washing dishes at the kitchen sink, the stink of a paper mill, the chill of a waiting room where anything might happen and usually does, the cadences of language and variances of human attitude, glimpsed up-close or slant. All the things around us, physical and atmospheric, obvious or implied, combine to center, guide, and sharpen a writer's sensibilities, leaving impressions that endure.

Which is probably why, when I take myself to the most generic and mundane of places—a car dealership in Greensboro—I find an inkling of story. I am not even looking for a story, but closely observed, any place can become a particular place and will attract stories.

Stories begin in a "where." There's got to be a where before somebody shows up and things begin to happen. Once a character arrives on the scene, she's bound by the laws of human nature to have some kind of reaction to her surroundings. Place is a medium, after all, a kind of situational petri dish that cultures behavior, good, bad, or indifferent. The nature of place is that it insists upon being reckoned with by *everyone*, not just writers.

At the car dealership, it's 7:30 A.M.; there's a complimentary pot of superheated coffee-turned-to-sludge, the sort of beverage that threatens to melt any cup you pour it into. Florescent lighting bleaches the air. I can't tolerate the inane blather of TV ads in the lounge area. The mechanic has told me the inspection might take an hour and a half. I've brought some reading, and so I amble around the glacial showrooms stocked with cars so pristine, so quietly muscular, they look embalmed, mosey past a warren of mostly empty offices, until I locate a dark and distant room where I trespass. There's a white board scribbled with statistics. "One out of four demos *will* buy," reads one note. Ah! Secret information! This is a room where car salesmen are trained. I sit down at the seminar table, settle in, flip open my book. Then, a woman pokes her head into the room. She, too, is seeking asylum from the infernal TV. "Mind if I join you?" she asks in a honey-baked down-home accent. "I need some place I can read my Bible in peace."

She lugs in a Bible as big as a cinderblock and sits across from me. Her lips move silently as her fingers glide down a page. The incongruity of a woman devotedly reading her Bible in proximity to the sleek, glossy, secular showroom of a car dealership resonates. I'm suddenly wide awake and loving that I'm in this place, where sharky commerce and somebody's faith so blithely coexist. Would I be so attuned to the dynamics of incongruity if I lived elsewhere? If many of my elders had not been drawling North Carolina porch-sitters who made mountains out of molehills and thrived on the odd detail? Maybe. What I do know is that my upbringing in such a story-centric milieu accelerates my delight in such gleanings, has honed my appetite for, my appreciation *and* expectation of them. I have learned to keep vigil for stories. A place might seem as ordinary as a still pond waiting for ripples, but if you keep watching and listening like a patient fisherman, the ripples *will* come. A fish *is* going to leap out of the water—or something even more extraordinary. Even the hucksterish, generic chic of a car dealership can glitter with more than chrome.

How important is place in a writer's life? Very. But a writer can write anywhere, right? Writing's the portable art—all one needs is a pencil and paper, or an electronic tablet. While it's true that the act of writing can happen anywhere, without the writer imagining a place in which a work is grounded, the story drifts, unmoored. Place, both on the page and in life, is about location, a solid sensory somewhere, belonging to it or not belonging, feeling niched or agitating to be elsewhere. What do all writers who have lived in North Carolina have in common? Time spent soaking up the sensations of this place and possibly feeling inspired. Is there evidence that affiliation with North Carolina contributed in some way to each writer's development or vision or craft or sensibilities? Absolutely.

When I wrote to potential contributors about the *Amazing Place* project, my hunch was that every writer would have something to say about the role North Carolina has played in his or her writing life. Some would tell their stories more forthrightly or chronologically than others, addressing the specifics of how North Carolina nurtured their growth as writers. Some would write a more oblique response. But my main prompt—from which branched other more-inclusive prompts to give writers as much creative latitude as I felt they needed—went something like this: We seem to have a lot of writers here. Why? How does living in North Carolina matter? How is living in North Carolina conducive to the writing life? If a writer lived here for a time but left, what part of North Carolina does he or she carry forever? What memories of certain North Carolina places and the people who inhabited them persist to the extent that a writer must allow for their influence or inspiration? How has some specific "where" in North Carolina served as muse? These are the rather open-ended questions I asked contributors to this book to consider. And they responded in delightfully variant ways.

Amazing Place is a book of personal narratives, not "essays." I've found that sometimes the word "essay" scares readers (and writers) away. Of course it shouldn't. But I myself tend to hear the word "essay" and associate it with the kind of densely formal, buttoned-down prose that tends, as I read it, to make my eyelids heavy. In contrast, the personal narratives gathered here are more like "stories," meant to entertain as well as enlighten. Although no featherweights of truth, information, and insight, they are by turns meditative, breezy, confessional, cranky, self-reflective, investigative, conversational, whimsical, humorous, sly, factual, wistful, brave—and sometimes all of the above at once. They are written with the heart and gusto of writers who like surprising themselves as much as their readers, of writing toward an idea with little clue of what they themselves will dig up along the way. Ultimately, what makes each narration resolutely *personal* is the distinct personality of the author conveyed through tone and style. Readers of *Amazing Place* can expect what fans of North Carolina literature most admire: the wizardry and welter of original, resonant voices telling fine tales. These tales happen to be true. Think of this book as a travelogue of muses, taking us to specific "somewheres" that have impacted each writer's imagination.

I have included as contributors both well-established and emerging (or less familiar) writers of prose. They are diverse in gender, race, age, and regional association (mountains, piedmont, coastal plain). Some are newcomers to the state—Belle Boggs and Stephanie Elizondo Griest write about that experience, examining the nature of belonging itself. Boggs wonders if she'll ever feel sufficiently familiar in her new Chatham County home to call herself a North Carolina writer. But she has begun to discover the flora and fauna native to the surrounding countryside and write about it, and she delights in imagining her new daughter as a North Carolinian by birth. Griest, a Mexican American from Texas and world traveler who has never alighted any place for long, contemplates the joys of having found a writing home in Carrboro that will nourish and restore. How welcomed her nomadic muse feels to have landed in a place where men of all ages call her "Ma'am" and women call her "Honey," where deer roam and butterflies hover. But will she lose her "urban edge"? Rosecrans Baldwin married a native North Carolinian, lived in Chatham County for a few years, but recently vamoosed for professional reasons. Baldwin's are shrewdly observed confessions of political letdown and cultural bafflement experienced while a resident.

Having grown up in North Carolina, several contributors explore coming-of-age experiences that have informed their writing lives since. Lumberton native Jill McCorkle celebrates the sources of her writer's "voice," believing that stories begin with listening. "Sing yourself to where the singing comes from," she quotes from a poem by Seamus Heaney, a line she feels that describes the writing life and how our earliest sensory experiences in the places we were born shape both the beginnings of our imaginations and their destinies. "What I am as a writer I owe mostly to the good fortune of having been born and raised in North Carolina," writes Robert Morgan, who grew up in the hardscrabble mountains among great storytellers and the cadences of the King James Bible, but who also immersed himself in the physicality of that world: climbing, digging, catching rabbits, and knowing trees "like friends." His narrative documents his journey from a boyhood dream to write "something as powerful as a thunderstorm" to his writer's education by cherished mentors and friends. Randall Kenan takes us to his family farm in Chinquapin, describing days filled with "mosquitoes and roadkill," the deep poverty of neighbors, "a sense of lucklessness and a heavy dose of hard work." While he's working in a tobacco field during a thunderstorm, something happens that changes him forever and allows him to know what Eudora Welty meant when she wrote that "Place has a more lasting identity than we have." Michael McFee examines the nature of "relief" in an homage to his Buncombe County origins, suggesting multiple interpretations of the word. For instance, sometimes we understand a place better, with new fondness or regard, when we see it on a map, in relief. Did growing up in the mountains predispose him to write poetry? "The daily vertical movement of living at higher altitudes is not unlike the experience of writing a poem," he suggests. Pamela Duncan writes about reading the sorts of books that ultimately led her to understanding the power of writing about a place one knows well, beginning with her grandparents' "little red tarpaper house" in Black Mountain. Marianne Gingher considers the advantages, however dull her choice may seem, of living and writing in Greensboro, the town where she grew up.

Having spent his boyhood in Orange County, Wells Tower serves up an uproarious portrait of a neighborhood bully, a piece that conveys how place and character are intricately bound. With near reverence, Bland Simpson explores the enduring impact of the watery landscape Down East, not only on his nearly amphibious beginnings but his heart and soul as well. Transplant Jan DeBlieu writes about the irresistible wildness of the Outer Banks and the barnacle-like tenacity it took to make it her writing home. "Living here has made me wake up to my life," she writes. Landscapes of memory are explored with insight and tenderness in Judy Goldman's narrative about crossing a river to become a North Carolina writer. Ben Fountain pays haunting tribute to a patch of cherished and much-contested family land. To timber or not to timber was the crux of the squabble throughout his boyhood and beyond. "What was I doing out there all those years ago those mornings I spent traipsing around the woods behind the barns?" he writes, recollecting the vast jungle green of the place. Perhaps, he speculates, he was finding a "version of grace."

From west to east, the art of storytelling, distinctions among regional dialects, the picayune differences between fact and true fact, and the musicality of tales are the focus of native writers Fred Chappell, Clyde Edgerton, and Michael Parker. "Pith and vinegar, that is the character of the speech habits of North Carolinians in the blue-and-green hills," Chappell claims. Digression, memory piled on memory, "the memories of memories (sometimes reshaped a little, sometimes a lot) . . . like a wisteria vine through pines" characterize Edgerton's narrative about a family graveyard and, by admission, his writer's craft. Writing about the long-winded tale his father tells at dinner, a story that "begins to resemble a map of those got-to-go-around-your-ass-to-get-to-your-elbow roads," Parker recollects hearing in his father's opening lines "that sweet, slow, soulful music of home," which, for him, is the essence of style.

According to Monique Truong, a young refugee from Vietnam whose family settled in Boiling Springs, North Carolina's influence began with a book her father gave her titled *North Carolina Parade: Stories of People and History*, and she clung to this book like a life raft floating her between countries. What did acquiring a college degree in North Carolina teach the writer that she hadn't known before? Jenny Offill and Lydia Millet address the question in a lively, frank conversational exchange about the writing classes they took at UNC. In Will Blythe's meditative piece, the writer's muse plays tag with life and death as he parses "where" from "nowhere." From his earliest inklings of mortality during a lush Chapel Hill boyhood until coming to terms with his mother's death in a Chapel Hill cemetery, he identifies key elements of place that not only vivify his past but, as is a writer's prerogative, transform the ordinary into legend: cicadas, boxwoods lit with fireflies, pinecones, and magical sticks. "That a stick in a Carolinian backyard can become what you wish it . . . that's the making of poetry before you even know what poetry is," Blythe writes.

Contributors could write about anything so long as North Carolina served as backdrop or place of reckoning: family, jobs, mentors, communities, books read, vistas, risks, opportunities, craft, language, habits, disappointments, fears, revelations, strife, and joys. Lee Smith, in her delightful and touching piece, "Salad Days," writes with signature charm about all of the above in a paean to the town of Chapel Hill.

For some, North Carolina as a place of hallowed ground or influence may be a distant memory; for others, it offers still a wellspring of daily curiosities and marvels. But if it was ever a writing home that held sway in a writer's imagination, it's worth returning to, if only on the page. It's likely (and often in the subtlest ways) that the remembered particulars of this place continue to serve the writer's muse wherever it roams. "But why had he always felt so strongly the magnetic pull of home," wrote Thomas Wolfe in *You Can't Go Home Again.* "Why had he thought so much about it and remembered it with such blazing accuracy, if it did not matter . . . ?"

MARIANNE GINGHER
CHAPEL HILL, 2014

The Mountains

Fertile North Carolina

ROBERT MORGAN

What I am as a writer I owe mostly to the good fortune to have been born and raised in North Carolina. Almost all my poetry and fiction is set in the mountains in the western part of the state, and the voices I have heard and written belong to the Old North State and the southern highlands.

I have been asked many times by people in the North why there are so many outstanding writers associated with North Carolina. The flippant answer is: because there ain't nothing else to do down there. But the more serious answer is: because of Thomas Wolfe. Once Wolfe became such a celebrated writer and international celebrity, and his fiction made such an impact on young readers, inspiring passionate admirers, it was inevitable that the talented youth of North Carolina would think of following his career path. The state became, from the 1930s on, a seedbed and hotbed for young writers, and UNC–Chapel Hill was the forcing house.

But there are many other factors besides the fame of Thomas Wolfe that have contributed to the bumper crop of writers from North Carolina over the years. When I was a student at N.C. State University in 1962–63, Sam Ragan had a feature in the *Raleigh News and Observer* every Sunday celebrating one North Carolina author or another, usually with pictures and an interview. It was obvious that writers were important and recognized in the state.

A few years ago, I was interviewed on the farm where I grew up on Green River in Henderson County. The reporter looked at the cornfield and old barn and said, "Tell me, I'm curious, how did you ever get from here to Cornell University,

because practically speaking, you can't get there from here."
I told him I could understand why he would ask that question. After all, my parents were poor, without a lot of formal education. We didn't have a car or truck or tractor. We plowed our land with a horse and kept our milk and butter in the springhouse when I was small. But in fact I had some distinct advantages for a future writer.

I grew up among great storytellers. My grandpa had a thousand stories about ghosts and panthers, snakes and mad dogs, bears, haunted places. We talked on the porch in summer and by the fire in winter. He sent us to bed many times terrified by his yarns of panthers coming down chimneys, snakes long as a man was tall. He'd polished those tales over his lifetime. My dad had gone only to the sixth grade in school, but he was an avid reader. He subscribed to the *National Geographic Magazine*, and he read history and biography. He had absorbed an enormous amount of history from his grandfather, who was a veteran of the Confederate army and Elmira prison camp. My dad had an extraordinary memory for detail and loved to tell about George Washington at Valley Forge and Daniel Boone in Kentucky, Teddy Roosevelt on San Juan Hill. I drank in his stories and acquired a love of history from him. He could make the past come alive. My mother was a gifted talker also, preferring stories about witches, babies marked in the womb, women charmed by rattlesnakes. It was she who told me the many family stories about Gap Creek and the old days on Mount Olivet where my Grandma Levi had grown up.

I was also fortunate to explore the woods and fields and pastures around our house. My great grandpa, Daniel Pace, had bought a square mile of land on Green River in 1838, and I knew virtually every foot of it, from the riverbank to the top of the mountain. I built ponds on the pasture branch, dug caves in the walls of the gully, caught rabbits in a rabbit gum, and slid on a plank on leaves down the mountainside. I knew the weeds and thickets, the different kinds of soils and clays, the rocks and sinkholes. I climbed the trees, and knew trees like friends. That sense of intimacy with the place is so strong I have compared every other place I've seen to it, to this day.

Every day we read the Bible aloud, and I was exposed to the majesty of the King James Scripture. We attended church and prayer meetings four times a week and sang hymns and gospel songs. From the first, I loved music. When I was two or three and resisted taking a nap, all my mother had to do was sit down and start singing. It could be any song at all, a hymn, carol, Stephen Foster. As soon as I heard the first note, I dropped whatever I was doing and ran to her lap. Pressing my cheek to her breast, I could hear the voice through the flesh, and the measure of her heartbeat. Every time, I floated away into an arcadia of melody and dreams.

As I got older, I listened to the radio, to church choirs, country music, Christmas carols, and even classical music. Longines watches sponsored the Philadelphia Orchestra every Sunday afternoon, and I thrilled to the grandeur of that polyphony. I made up music in my head to accompany whatever I was doing. It was tunes based on what I had heard. One special tune I played in my head over and over. Only years later did I discover that it came from Bach's Fifth Brandenburg.

My parents read to me as an infant, and my mother taught me to read before I ever went to school. I was always interested in reading and writing. As I grew older, I wanted to write something grand, an epic poem, an oratorio, grand as the Cicero Mountain across the river. I wanted to write something as powerful as a thunderstorm or the procession of the seasons. I wanted to find language radiant as sunlight on pine needles.

Two wonderful things happened to me the year I was in the sixth grade. I had Dean Ward, principal of Tuxedo Elementary School, as a teacher, and the Henderson County bookmobile began coming to Green River Baptist Church every first Monday afternoon of the month. Mr. Ward was a relative who had grown up on Bob's Creek and gone off to Chapel Hill. He also was a wonderful storyteller, and regaled us with stories of the old days, of the Roaring Twenties, ancient history, the plots of *The Iliad* and *The Odyssey, Silas Marner, Paradise Lost.* He drilled us in grammar and for the first time, I began to have a firmer sense of the structure of language. I became self-conscious about the way I spoke, the way I pronounced words. I will never forget my first sight of the bookmobile. It was an old utility truck outfitted with bookshelves. I'd never seen so many books. There I discovered *Farmer Boy* and *Little House on the Prairie.* I soon graduated to Jack London's *Call of the Wild* and James Oliver Curwood's novels of the Royal Canadian Mounted Police and the Far North. In the future I would discover Thomas Wolfe's *Look Homeward, Angel* there and *War and Peace.* I was so enthralled by Wolfe's story, I thought I was Eugene Gant and his family were my family. I knew he had grown up in Asheville thirty miles away, and I began to think that if Wolfe could write a book about Asheville and sell it to Yankees, maybe I could write something and get it published.

But while in Mr. Ward's class, I was discovering Jack London and James Oliver Curwood. I enjoyed those books so much I slipped them inside textbooks and read them in class. Once Mr. Ward caught me reading *White Fang* while he was up lecturing. Instead of scolding me, he lifted the book out of my hands and laid it on the shelf above the radiator.

In the spring of 1957, the fifth grade took a trip to the Biltmore House, George Vanderbilt's unlikely chateau near Asheville. The excursion cost three dollars, which I did not have. I stayed in the classroom while the others went. Mr. Ward looked at me sitting at the desk and said he didn't want me to waste the day. He knew I liked to read those novels about the northern wilderness. He told me I should write a story, and he would give me a plot: a man is lost in the Canadian Rockies. He doesn't have a gun or a knife. Describe how he survives and returns to civilization.

I remember staring at the white sheet of paper in front of me and wondering how to write a story. Recognizing that I

ROBERT MORGAN

14

did not know how to write a story, I decided to make up some details about how the man survives. I wrote that he sharpened a stick on a rock to make a spear, and rubbed sticks together to start a fire. He fitted a worm on a thorn for a fish hook, and followed a stream to the lower elevations. I got so involved in making up plausible details that I was surprised when the other students returned from the Biltmore House. And I had written my first story.

When I was sixteen, I wanted to be many things. I wanted to compose music, and I wanted to study science and mathematics. I wanted to attend West Point, and I wanted to build highways. As it turned out, I attended N.C. State University to study aerospace engineering and applied mathematics. In those day we were supposed to do our part in beating the Russians in the space race. I wanted to be a rocket scientist.

I had been writing all along, and I had entered college without graduating from high school. My first encounter with a writer happened that fall of 1962 when I attended a workshop taught Monday evenings by the playwright and actor Romulus Linney. Anyone could attend, and I listened to Rom talk about his work in the theater, as well as fiction writing. He sometimes brought famous writers to the class, including Reynolds Price and Edward Albee. It was from Rom Linney that I first got some idea about how a professional writer might speak and act. Things were going so well in my math classes I decided to accelerate and take an advanced class in differential equations. My advisor looked at my transcript and said, "Why, you never graduated from high school." He refused to let me accelerate. I was disappointed, but discovered I could take English 222, Creative Writing, in the time slot freed up. The professor was the novelist Guy Owen.

Owen's class was so much fun I began to think less and less about differential equations and the Bernoulli Principle and more about how to write a decent English sentence. Guy Owen said things the first day of the class that I'm still passing on to my students. He said learn to use the precise names for

Fertile North Carolina

things. Don't say tree, say oak tree, or better yet chestnut oak or water oak. (This is what Henry James called "solidity of specification.") He told us to listen to the way people actually speak, to get the living inflections that will make a character come alive in dialogue and narration.

About the third or fourth week of the semester, I gave Guy a little story I'd written about my great-grandmother Delia Johnson Capps. As a little girl in 1862, she had been taken out of the dangerous mountains of North Carolina to Walter-boro, South Carolina, to be safe. She was safe there until Sherman's army reached Savannah and turned north, devastating central South Carolina. She could remember bodies being piled on their porch, and dogs climbing up on the bodies licking the blood.

Guy brought the story into class and said he wept when he read it. None of my math teachers had said anything like that to me. I was hooked on writing and never looked back. I began to think less about the space race and more about the textures and power of words.

Transferring to UNC–Chapel Hill in 1963, I intended to study both literature and pure mathematics, and write fiction. But I soon fell in with a group of students from the Northeast who were obsessed with contemporary poetry. They had been kicked out of the finest prep schools in New England, and they had come south to be beatniks and poets. They could talk about French poetry, metaphor, line breaks, and William Butler Yeats. They knew a great deal more than I did about poetry. We lived and breathed poetry that year. I read Robert Lowell, James Wright, Gary Snyder, and many others.

In the fall of 1964, several things happened that deeply influenced my writing. I became aware of the sound of words, the textures of words, the resonance of words, in a new way. I saw a shaft of sunlight break through the clouds after a storm and thought of a timber of light bracing the sky. I wrote a haiku-like poem about that beam, my first authentic effort in poetry. And one day in my room on Rosemary Street, while reading T. S. Eliot's "Burnt Norton" aloud, I realized that poetry was made of beautiful sentences broken into lines. That may seem pretty obvious now, but then it was a revelation. I began to write more and more poems.

The most talented of my poet friends from the North was named Dudley Carroll. He asked me to show him some of the stuff I was writing. Unsure of myself, I held back. Finally, I did type up some of the short things I'd been working on and hand them to him. At two or three o'clock in the morning there was a knock on my door. Half-awake, I opened the door, and there stood Dudley and his friend Tim Perkins. Dudley was almost shaking with excitement. "These poems are so good we had to come tell you," he said. No honor I have ever received, no best-seller list, has meant more to me than his surprising enthusiasm. I worked on poetry with a new confidence.

At the same time, I was taking a writing class with the fiction writer Jessie Rehder. Jessie was having problems with alcohol, but she was a wonderful, generous teacher, and I wrote both poems and stories for her class. One day I was crossing the parking lot to the Wilson Library and she was driving out of the lot. She stopped her car, rolled down the window, and said, "You're the most talented writer I've ever taught," then drove away. She may have said that to all her students for all I know, but I walked on into the library that day about three feet off the ground.

The MFA program in writing had been started at UNC–Greensboro, and it was my good fortune to study there in 1967–68. Writers, not scholars, were the stars in that English department, a tradition started by Allen Tate and Randall Jarrell. I was lucky to work with both Robert Watson and Fred Chappell. Each wrote both fiction and poetry, as I did. I soon discovered that Fred Chappell was the best reader of poetry I had ever encountered.

Because I was married and had a child and held two part-time jobs, I was excused from most of the workshops. Instead, I would meet Fred for tutorials. I would give him poems, and we met every week or two at a café called the Pickwick in late afternoon to go over the work I had submitted. Fred's erudition, his critical eye, his generosity and enthusiasm were inspiring. I remember thinking, "He really understands how these poems are written." The honesty of the man was impressive. I began to concentrate more and more on poetry, and less on fiction. And I began to get some sense of my own voice and subject matter. Fred was from Haywood County, in the mountains, and he knew the world and the voices I knew.

I believe a poet cannot come into his or her own until he or she has a true reader, an authentic reader. That is why poets and writers so often come in pairs and clusters: Wordsworth and Coleridge, Goethe and Schiller, Emerson and Thoreau, Byron and Shelly, Faulkner and Sherwood Anderson, Elizabeth Bishop and Marianne Moore. For me, Fred was the true reader. All you need is one, and I was damn lucky to find him at UNC–Greensboro.

I owe a great deal to North Carolina and the people who taught me and encouraged me, the land there, the blue valleys and mountains, the rich soil of the bottomlands, the waterfalls and remote coves, the people who wrung a living from the rocky ridges, the ancient hunting ranges of the Cherokees. When I was a boy hoeing corn, I often turned up arrowheads and pieces of Indian pottery. It seemed the ground itself was haunted by the Cherokees and the Indians who had come before them. It was a world brimming with history, with poetry, with stories. It was my legacy, waiting to be written down.

ROBERT MORGAN

Our First Steps

MONIQUE TRUONG

*"[T]he true birthplace is . . . [where] for the first time one looks
intelligently upon oneself. My first homelands have been books."*
—Marguerite Yourcenar

*"[W]hatever is on the outside can be taken away at any time.
Only what is inside you is safe."*
—Jeanette Winterson (on why she memorizes books)

In 1976, my father gave me a hardcover book entitled *North
Carolina Parade: Stories of History and People*, coauthored by
Richard Walser and Julia Montgomery Street, with illustrations by Dixie Burrus Browning. The publisher was the University of North Carolina Press, and the publication date was
1966. My father must have purchased *North Carolina* used,
as an inside corner of the dust jacket had been snipped and
the price, $5.50, was written in pencil near the edge of the
missing triangle. I do not remember any secondhand book-
stores in Boiling Springs, North Carolina, where we lived at
the time, or even in nearby Shelby, the county seat of Cleve-
land County and a metropolis in comparison. I was only eight
years old in 1976, but I was already careful to note the places
where books could be found because books had become my
telescope through which other worlds could be glimpsed and
observed and, more importantly, where other life forms might
be found.

I have carried this *North Carolina* with me to all the states
where I have lived since: Ohio, Texas, Connecticut, California,
and New York. In order to understand the import and sub-

stance of this book in my life, you must understand that for me, land is not synonymous with home. I believe unequivocally that land is unimportant, even though we humans continue to fight for control over it, drawing borders and violating them. Home, on the other hand, is a potent idea, and ideas can be documented and chronicled in books and, better still, can live, thrive, and remain safe inside of you.

I know for certain the year when my father gave me *North Carolina* because he wrote "1976" on the page opposite to the one where he wrote this in red ink:

> *To my daughter Monique,*
> *to know about the state where we made our first steps*
> *to freedom.*
> *Daddy*

Then, for good measure and perhaps to assert his personhood beyond his relationship to me, he added his signature, which resembled a cardiogram of a racing heart or an unbroken line tracing the contour of a vertiginous mountain range. Soon after this, he would change his signature to one that was far more readable with neatly formed letters, so that at a quick glance you would know that this man was named Charles Truong. In 1976, he was not so forthcoming or easy to decipher, and that was the man who gave me *North Carolina*.

"Our first steps" actually took place the year before.

On April 30, 1975, the Vietnam War ended when North Vietnamese troops entered Saigon, South Vietnam, the city and country where I was born. Days before, my mother and I had departed from there in secret inside the belly of a military transport plane, the kind that swallowed jeeps like insects. My father left on April 30 in the maw of a boat, which became a child's toy on the open seas. That was the bargain he had made with his employer, a Dutch-owned oil company, and the U.S. government. The U.S. Embassy in Saigon would ensure our safe departure, and my father would remain to oversee the distribution of fuel to a lost military cause. I cannot imagine making this bargain.

It would be a fiction to claim or to believe that my father chose Boiling Springs as the site for our first home in this country. A military contractor, whom my father had worked with in South Vietnam, lived in Boiling Springs, and that man chose us. In fact, he sponsored us, which meant that he had pledged to a nongovernmental agency that he would (or ensure that other individuals or entities would) provide us with food, clothing, and shelter until we became self-sufficient. Without his "sponsorship," we would not have been able to leave our respective relocation centers, which were, in fact, repurposed military bases. My mother and I were in Camp Pendleton in California, and my father was in Fort Chaffee in Arkansas. By summer's end, we were all in Boiling Springs in a rented trailer home, sorting through plastic bags full of donated clothes and boxes brimming with canned goods that had been collected by the local churches for The Refugee Family, which was our collective identity then. I did not understand that we were lucky to be there. I only understood my new surroundings and life as a diminishment of what I had known before. The trailer home was a sliver of the riverfront villa, one of two houses where my family had lived. The clothes had been worn by someone else and looked and sometimes smelled as if they had been. The contents of the cans were unrecognizable to me as food.

This is what I brought with me to Boiling Springs: two languages, Vietnamese and French. The former I already could read and write. The latter was a foundational vocabulary for my first "second language." Soon, I traded in both for fluency in English. My father and mother already had English among their three languages. Again, I did not understand that we were fortunate in more than one way.

That, perhaps, was why my father gave me *North Carolina*. He knew that history or rather the knowledge of history was the beginning of context, and thus was the beginning of what the Belgian author Marguerite Yourcenar had described as "look[ing] intelligently upon oneself." Perhaps, he also observed that books provided me with solace. The only Asian child in Boiling Springs, I had become a ghost of a girl. I was silent, almost mute. I had a new language, but I had no one to speak it with. Instead, I searched books for friends, invisible except for the words that formed them.

I am certain that I immediately read all 209 pages of *North Carolina* because I read everything at that age. I was hungry for stories. I devoured books. In fact, I feared that there were a finite number of books in the world ("the world" was defined then as my local library), and that soon I would exhaust the supply. The first of *North Carolina*'s thirty-two short chapters was devoted to Virginia Dare, who, according to the authors, was "the first child of English parents to be born in America" in 1587, on Roanoke Island, off the coast of what would become the state of North Carolina. Nine days after Dare's birth, she and her parents, along with the ninety-eight other adults in the colony, vanished, leaving behind nothing but subsequent speculations about their tragic end at the hands of Native Americans. Collectively, they became known as the Lost Colony, but it was Dare's small, fragile body that became the stand-in for the entirety of the mystery and the enormity of the loss.

I did not recognize the clear function of Virginia Dare's story when I first read it on the opening pages of *North Carolina* nor later when it was taught to me in my classes at Boiling Springs Elementary. Virginia Dare was a creation myth. She was a sacrificial innocent, and her presumably spilled blood gave birth to all that was to come, which was the state of North Carolina and, even more importantly, North Carolinians. They, which now included me, were born of hope, determination, and the promise of the New World.

On December 25, 1975, an ice-and-snow storm transformed the western and central counties of North Carolina into a

landscape that I had only seen in books. Every tree branch—
I remember even the tree trunks themselves—wore a thick
wavy coat of ice. Glistening icicles hung from the eaves and
the rain gutters of houses, including the single-story brick
building, Spartan and barrack-like, that was our apartment
on Oak Street. (The rented trailer home had succumbed to
one of the most common fates that plagues these containers
of people: an electrical fire.)

My mother stuffed me into two pairs of pants, multiple
sweaters, a winter coat, a knit hat and gloves, too many pairs
of socks, and waterproof boots—every item donated and the
wrong size, but I was grateful for the first time to have them.
I ran out onto a small rectangular yard covered with snow,
the first that I had ever seen, touched, and soon tasted. I
also heard the snow, a faint crackling, because it was already
slowly, imperceptibly melting. Pure joy for me will always be
accompanied by that soundscape.

On July 2, 1976, the city of Saigon and the country of South
Vietnam disappeared altogether from the official maps. The
victors of a war change the names of conquered places because it is the most expedient way to deny their former inhabitants of the hope of return, no matter whether they had fled
or stayed in place. "There is no there there," as Gertrude Stein
had noted about her own childhood city of Oakland, California, within decidedly peacetime context but with the same
forceful acknowledgment to a disappearance and erasure.

There was only the New World now. Perhaps, this was another reason that my father gave me *North Carolina*.

The book is here with me now, and my father is not. The last
time I heard his voice was in North Carolina, near High Point.
My husband and I were in a rental car on our way back to New
York City. It was September 14, 2001.

On the night of September 10, we had flown down to Atlanta, Georgia, for a press conference scheduled for the following morning to unveil an advertising campaign that my hus-

band's company had developed, which would have turned the tunnels of MARTA, the city's transit system, into billboards with moving images. Instead, we awoke in our hotel room to the incomprehensible images of the Twin Towers collapsing. The local television stations in Atlanta were broadcasting the live feed from their counterparts in New York City. We recognized the faces of the news correspondents, but we could not understand anything that they were saying. All day long, we stood in front of television sets that replayed the same slow motion footage, and still we could not truly understand in words or in images what had happened to our home.

I was born in Saigon, South Vietnam, in 1968, while bombs cratered that city like it was the moon. Even before I was born, I experienced fear as the quickening of my mother's heartbeats and the tensing of every muscle in her body. I lived the first six years of my life in a country at war. I would hear with my own small body the sounds and feel the vibrations of organized violence, which is what war is even if you deem the war as "just" or "civil." Every war or act of war is a failure of the human spirit and of the imagination. Every war lives on in the body as a memory of this loss, and yet I could not reconcile that past with the present.

My father's voice on the cell phone sounded very far away that day. He was calling me from his home in Houston, Texas, where he would pass away in February of the following year. We were not in the habit of speaking to each other on the phone. We sent letters and then we e-mailed. He wrote to me in a formal English, and we were most comfortable sharing our thoughts in that language and these written modes of communication.

As High Point, North Carolina, passed by our car windows like a slide show, my father, in his British-accented English, said that he was glad that my husband and I were safe. He said that what happened on September 11 would be the beginning of another war. He sounded exhausted, though it was we who had driven nonstop for hours, counterintuitively trying to return as quickly as possible to a city that now had another name: Ground Zero. What my father did not have to say was that the New World was like the old one, and that now he had no other state to give me.

100

FRED CHAPPELL

100 is a noble number. Think *centurion,* think *century plant,* think *C-note.* Think of the algebra test on which you made a perfect score.

I never scored so heroically. In fact, I roundly flunked high school algebra. But I did harbor an aspiration. 100 is a number able to inspire the susceptible temperament to attempt tall undertakings and to sprint toward shining goals.

North Carolina is divided into 100 counties. I once formed, or was victim of, an ambition to write a sort of historical-fictional atlas of my home state. I would write 100 short stories, each of them set in a different county and in a different time period. The project, though huge, would be fun to labor upon. Especially enticing was the reading required. I imagined all the authored histories to be perused, all the oral histories to be attended, all the archives and artifacts to be fondled, all the necessary jaunts to historic homes, hamlets, and hollers.

Attacking this grandiose scheme, I managed to write one — count 'em, *one* — short story. It was called "Thatch Retaliates"; it took place during colonial times in the town of Bath in the county of Beaufort. It told of the infamous pirate Blackbeard (birth name, Edward Thatch or Teach) and his sneaking, murderous attack upon an innocent traveler. A longish time was required to write the story and more effort than I had counted on. When I finished setting it down, the number 100 began to recede in my mind at a great rate of speed, like a barely glimpsed comet spurting through our solar system.

I was too old for that sort of ambition. I was in my thirties when I wrote the Blackbeard tale. To write 100 such narratives is the dream of boys and girls of twenty or so. It is the ambition of a foolhardy youth to date every girl in his alma mater's Kappa Delta sorority, to perform Mendelssohn's Violin Concerto on the eve of receiving his M.D., of reading every last book in the university library at Chapel Hill. Thomas Wolfe owns to this latter ambition in *Look Homeward, Angel*, and if anyone was ever going to accomplish the feat, he was the man to do it.

He never accomplished it, but I think he came closer to his goal than I did to mine. The source of inspiration was the same for both of us: the grand, wide, long, high, and deep vistas of opportunity. The history of North Carolina offers every sort of attractive material for writers: personalities like Zebulon Vance and Wolfe himself, battles scattered through dozens of wars large and small, fascinating women like Dolley Madison and Ava Gardner and Wilma Dykeman, daring ventures like those of the Wright brothers and Sir Walter Raleigh, and the less coruscating but wonderfully significant lives of millers, ministers, and moonshiners.

Even now, as I set down this abrupt, small list, I feel an urge to plunder my shelves and begin making notes. Maybe 100 is not so daunting a count as it seems.

Yes it is. By now I can pretty well estimate my limits, and my failing at my aborted project is one reason I am able to do so.

The trouble is, North Carolina is many places, and most of us can know only a few of them well enough to write about. Wolfe knew the mountains well and treated them beautifully; he knew the piedmont area pretty well and treated it in a more than satisfactory fashion. The eastern counties he hardly touched upon, and I have wondered if he might not find that area as strange as New York City. He wrote about the Big Apple rather as a tourist might write in letters to his sister back home in Spruce Pine.

I share his shortcomings in trying to write about eastern

North Carolina. I have set stories in Paris, Vienna, London, and in a fairy-tale pseudo-Renaissance Italy, among other far-flung sites, and have managed to scrape through mainly by fashioning narratives in which the sense of place was much less important than the situations and characters.

But N.C. East confuses me. The atmosphere of that part of the state seems that of a mostly vanished plantation culture with which I feel no kinship. When I visit small towns like Pleasant Hill and Comfort, I am never *entirely* at ease.

Day to day, I plug along satisfactorily in Greensboro in the piedmont. It is not so demanding a milieu as the mountains, nor so caste-bound as the sandhills and points east. The piedmont is solidly bourgeois, its placid monotony freshened by the smell of pine forests and the babble of universities.

North Carolina is like Caesar's Gaul only in the fact that it is divided into three parts. The divisions are first of all topographical and ecological, and those two factors have largely determined the historical and cultural partitions that appeared over a comparatively short period of time.

Where you have cultural and historical divisions, you have conflict, mostly in the matter of the manners and mores of daily habitude. You have what amounts to a class system, a theme upon which so much of British literature rears of its candlelit ramparts of ballrooms and drawing rooms. Let us imagine that a young blade, the son of a burley farmer in Haywood County, wins an athletic scholarship to the university in Chapel Hill. There he meets a girl whose parents own Willoughby Plantation in Windsor. They fall in love, these young'uns, but the boy finds that the girl's parents regard him with suspicion, especially after they discover that he is not even an Episcopalian.

Calling Jane Austen ...

On the Willoughby Plantation resides a Redbone hound named Beauregard. Should the prospective suitor reveal that his family hound is a Plott named Bocephus? East of Raleigh, the canine name Bocephus is enunciated only in embarrassed whispers. West of Marion, Bocephus is likely to have a beagle porch mate named Booger.

In the piedmont, your nothin'-but-a hound will be called Elvis.

Dog names are but a single example of the details that signal slight cultural differences. Complicated episodes of *Downton Abbey* are built upon equally small differences, and the writers are able to find engaging drama in them.

Here is another imaginary scenario, this one historical and entailing a more interior kind of conflict than the courtship dilemma.

Two brothers who grew up together in Biscoe in the sandhills had to part company when the younger found employment in a rayon factory in Enka, twenty miles west of Asheville. The older remained on the family farm with its peach orchards. A decade passed, and during that period it happened that President Lyndon B. Johnson decided it was worth losing the party support of southern states in the interest of racial equity. One of the brothers embraced the president's decision, the other did not.

Chekhov would have relished this situation. His novella would be titled "Peaches," referring to the custom of the farmer brother to ship a gift bushel westward every August. The heart of Chekhov's story would be a trenchant scene in which most of the dialogue went unspoken.

In mountain country houses a flatiron is heated, along with two others, on the top of a wood-burning kitchen range. When the farmwife irons clothes, she trades off as the iron employed grows cool. In the east, flatiron is the name of an expensive steak. In the piedmont, it is a building in the city.

Easterly, a coffeepot may be set to rest on a *trivet*. In Franklin County, it may sit on a *spider*. In the Research Triangle, it alights upon a *heat disperser*.

In the piedmont, a teenage driver who makes a fast and noisy start *guns it*. In the east, he *lays rubber*. In the hills, he *scratches off*.

In the mountains, a farmer *owes money*. In the east, he *incurs a debt*. A Charlotte banker has acquired *leverage*.

E: a woman may *sue for divorce*. P: a woman may *leave her husband*. W: husband and wife have only *separated*—often for decades.

Mountaineers wear eyeglasses; other Carolinians just wear glasses. This common redundancy is an Appalachian habit. "Raise the window up so we can get some air." "I bought me some funny-looking underwear pants." "Shut the window down before we freeze."

I do not adduce these wayward examples in the interest of language study. A licensed linguist or dialectologist might wish to have me arrested. These are merely notes, the sort of jottings I could make while trying to work out the dialogue of a story. Mark Twain and F. Scott Fitzgerald compiled similar materials, and probably scores of other writers follow the same practice.

To many readers, such minutiae must seem trivial, and in the interest of shaping large dramatic concepts they probably are trivial. But to a writer intent upon drawing a character who is both representative and nonrepresentative of her background and milieu, these small points are not petty. Her place and time in the world are partly defined by whether she is "going out" with a boy or "sparking" him.

If I may be indulged a couple of brief examples from my own pages, I will quote some dialogue passages from short stories I have been writing about a young fellow recently graduated from high school who comes to work for his uncle who owns a retail furniture company. The company is located in Tipton in the mountains west of Asheville, and the protagonist, Jerry, is from Down East, from a city something like New Bern. Jerry's work partner is Curly Spurling, an older and wiser man, humorous and tolerant, and a native of Tipton. Though Curly did not gain a high school degree, he serves in this situation as a mentor for Jerry.

One of the episodes is about deer hunting. The furniture company organizes an annual deer hunt for the male employees during Christmas season. Jerry, though a hunter himself, is curious about the mountaineer practice, and Curly tries to explain the local customs.

"I reckon it's what some people like to call tradition. . . . Somehow it just don't seem like the Christmas season unless you go out in the woods and shoot some animal that hadn't got the least idy of doing you any harm. Some people will hunt in the fields for rabbits, but they don't say they're aching to send cute little bunnies to hell. They say they've got to work their dogs to keep them in tone. That way it sounds like they're doing something useful and necessary. Some people will go squirrel hunting about this time, but the big thing is to go drop a deer which they think is all right because they're so big."

"How do you mean?" Jerry asked.

"Well, a squirrel is so little, it ain't hardly worth hunting down. You could just set out rat traps, if bagging them was the main thing. And a rabbit is a little varmint, too. But a deer is as big as you are, or bigger, so it is kind of like it's a fair fight."

"Except that the deer doesn't have a gun."

Curly eyed him curiously. "Why would you want to give a deer a gun? He couldn't hit the side of a hill."

In this passage from "Tradition," Jerry plays his usual role of naïve interlocutor and Curly plays the seasoned mountaineer. He uses Appalachian redundancy, "Christmastime season," the mordant mockery "to send cute little bunnies to hell," a local colloquialism, "to go *drop* a deer," and he shifts the focus of discussion with a tacit simile, that the deer hunting is a gun battle, which should be a fair fight. When Jerry objects, saying that the comparison is imperfect, Curly carries the mild joke into hyperbole: a deer with a rifle "couldn't hit the side of a hill." This latter phrase is proverbial and is often attached to a hunter whose skills are the subject of humor; the speaker's brother-in-law often bears the brunt.

I've written perhaps too many pages that rattle with this sort of dialogue. The mountaineer manner of talking is almost always dryly humorous, deeply skeptical, and often sardonic, hyperbolic, and indulgent of fleeting fantastic metaphors. I like and admire this way of speaking. To hear it has refreshed many a day's labor in the cornfield or along the drainage ditches or on the barn roof where the galvanized tin flashed and crackled in the August noon.

I recall once when with a country workmate named Buford Rhodes, I was painting the showroom of a supply store. We had to cover the ceiling with oil-based enamel paint. Rollers would not serve, so we had to climb on stepladders, holding the brushes above our heads. The smelly white paint ran off the bristles, onto the sticky brush handles, down under our short sleeves, and more than stingy amounts dripped into our faces and eyes. Nevertheless, Mr. Rhodes went at the task with determined cheerfulness, humming his peculiar version of "Wabash Cannonball." Suddenly he stopped to complain: "You know, this just ain't enough. I wish I had me a ceiling like this to paint that was a hundred yards wide and as long as from here to Clyde."

Was it sheer desperation that made that random lame remark seem so funny to me? I jumped down from the ladder and leaned against it, holding myself up while I laughed till tears diluted some of the paint on my cheeks.

It is not impossible to imagine other characters with darkly playful temperaments who speak in rough homespun and hold a sane sense of proportion about themselves. It is not impossible to place them in other situations. But the characters breathe more freely and see more perceptively in those places where they wish to belong. I recognize Jackson County natives easily when I encounter them in an airport bar in Utica or when they bear me about in a taxi in Chicago, but in these settings they are not exactly the same persons they were in North Carolina. They are less assured, a little defensive, a little less likely to open their minds. Perhaps they have become aware that their manner of speech sets them apart in their new surroundings.

Even though a writer hears a certain kind of talk appreciatively and may have grown up within its bounded area, he has no guarantee that he can put it down on paper in a convincing manner. That takes practice and, for me, more than a little revision.

The poet Kelly Cherry used to chide me about the way I talk. "Why do you say those hick things? You say 'ain't' and the department head 'don't know what he is doing,' and 'brung up ignorant,' and all that. It just sounds dumb. You would probably say, 'mighty dumb.'"

I explained that I wrote stories about my native hills and I spoke in that manner to keep dialogue patterns secure in aural memory. It was incumbent upon me to use a more formal mode of address while teaching in the classroom; I must flash proper English before my students. But I did not want to lose my ear for folk speech.

She was skeptical of my explanation. She may have thought I was only being ornery. To a certain measure, she may have been correct.

My orneriness would derive in part from an odd feeling of pride. I need not revisit here the annoyance some of us experience while reading *Snuffy Smith* in the newspaper comics or watching assorted film and television treatments. My friend Stuart Dischell teased me, saying I was much too sensitive on this point: "I don't see that the media are contemptuous of Appalachian people." My reply was a shade too exasperated for our casual discussion: "When do you think they'll produce a television show called 'The Beverly Wetbacks?'"

It may be that my excessively defensive attitude comes from my trying to have it both ways, from wishing to celebrate the traditions and folkways of my home ground while at the same time wishing that the culture I was born to was less provincial, less self-centered, and less suspicious than it is of the ways and motives of the rest of the world.

In the 1999 novel *Look Back All the Green Valley*, I took occasion to vent some frustration. The protagonist, Jess Kirkman, is traveling on family business from the piedmont to the mountains beyond Asheville. Along the way, impelled by curiosity, he stops for a meal at a chain restaurant called Hillbilly Heaven. The brief scene set in the eatery was designed to illustrate some of the insulting cultural clichés that have yoked to the idea of Appalachia. The restaurant menu lists such offerings as "Downhome Corneypones" and "Ticklish Tater Toes" and a "Nowhars Burger." ("You'll smack yore lips and say thar hain't nary a better burger nowhars.")

It is the drink menu that Jess finds most unsettling:

We've got the whistle-wetters you've been a-cravin' fer, neighbor. Jest don't tell the revenoors what we're up to! Only rock back and sip on one of our tasty specials! White Litenin'! This un's a double-vodka chocklit remedy with a sprig of cool-down mint. Mm-mm it'll hush up yer mug— 'ceptin' when you-uns holler fer more! B&B—that's right, folks, good ole bourbon and branch! But with a special secret spicin' we throw in fer free! Don't ask your server what it is 'cause she won't tell till the ole gray mare has kittens.

Now this sort of silly commercial caricature may be merely tacky, but Jess expects that it is bound to induce an irritated response from some customers. He learns from his server, however, that most of them are tolerant. She is identified by her name tag as "L'il Liza Jane." As he chats with her, Jess learns that she, Norma Wilson, is a student at Western Carolina University and may decide to concentrate upon folklore studies. She takes in stride the silliness of Hillbilly Heaven and reports that even the local native mountaineers find the place lightly amusing and do not take offence. She tells him

FRED CHAPPELL

34

that "all this hillbilly stuff gives the customers something to chat with me about."

The passage did not turn out as I had planned. It had seemed a good opportunity to insert in a mild-mannered novel a fiery philippic against the habitual disrespect of the media for minority subcultures. But as the episode unfolded in a fairly realistic way, I understood that my protagonist's attitude toward this perceived affront was overheated and would distract from the larger concerns of the story.

I had also to admit that, though it had been fun to compose the phony menu copy, I was only satirizing what was in itself a caricature, and that impartial readers must find tenuous interest in the subject, if they found any at all. I had struck a note too personal for the larger overview that fiction should provide.

When I try to list other cultural groups targeted by professional humorists and casual wiseacres, I soon run out of paper. Jews, African Americans, Amerindians, Latinos, evangelical Baptists, Mormons, WASPs—all of these and scores of other groups receive continual barrages of mean jokes and petty insults. So do certain professionals: politicians, dentists, preachers, umpires and referees, teachers, policemen, judges, priests and nuns and poets. Only bartenders seem to get off unscathed.

So, I must chastise myself for my overly tender delicacy in this matter and try to understand that any group or individual may unjustly receive contemptuous and disdainful treatment and that it is one of the duties of a writer to discover and promulgate fairness of judgment. To single out a certain economic class, cultural group, nation, religion, race, or gender as worthy of contumely is despicable. We Appalachians are not the only ones to endure unmannerly treatment, and we must protest the practice wherever, whenever it occurs.

Keeping these precepts firmly in mind, I have determined to retire to my closet and shut the door whenever I have the overpowering impulse to screech, revealing my innermost feelings and considered conviction, *"Texas sucks!"*

In view of the preceding paragraphs, it will be obvious to my readers that I am supremely unfitted to write 100 stories about North Carolina. The mountains have seized upon me and their spell is over me, no matter how long I may have to live elsewhere. Lee Smith spoke of meeting a gentleman who told her he did not desire to live in a place where he had no mountain to rest his eyes against. If I'd had his gift of the Appalachian tongue, I might have said the same thing. Lacking that gift, I shall no doubt parrot the saying and claim that it is original with me.

Pith and vinegar, that is the character of the speech habits of North Carolinians in the blue-and-green hills. But the humor has no flint and the import is heartless unless the sentences manage to discover a vein of unalloyed truth.

In "Tradition," the story quoted from a few pages ago, the narrative turned upon a hunting accident that almost killed a man. He was a victim of his own unsafe practices. Jerry had almost shot him, having been deceived by his movements in the underbrush. But he managed to lift his finger with the trigger just in time.

When he and Curly discuss the incident, the older man says, "Well, but the best part of your Christmas is over too."

"How come?"

"You done gave yourself the best present you'll ever have just by not pulling the trigger. Think about how it would be, every year people singing carols and talking about Santy Claus and you thinking about having kilt a man. Be the worst day of your life every twenty-fifth."

"It wouldn't be much fun."

"So—Merry Christmas!" Curly said. "And Happy New Year, too, if you don't shoot somebody by then."

"It'll be longer than January before I go hunting again," Jerry said. "It'll be a good little while."

"Don't wait too long or there won't be any deer left. No cows, either. These days, they're shooting everything a rifle can point at."

"They might shoot me."

"Not this year," Curly said. "In this county, the limit on human beings is one per season."

"How come?"

Curly squinted through the dusty windshield at the snow-dusted road ahead. The truck heater was not working today and his breath fogged the glass. "They're saving up the rest of us to make war with."

I like that final sentence so much that I'm pretty certain I didn't invent it. I must have recalled it. Or stolen it.

Anyhow, thank you, barn roof. Thank you, drainage ditches and hayfields. Thank you, tobacco patch. Thank you, Buford Rhodes.

The Stories That Lead Me Home

PAMELA DUNCAN

Most of my books start with a place, then a person.
The two have to be together. The place shapes the person.
—John Ehle

Long before I published my three novels (*Moon Women, Plant Life, The Big Beautiful*), even long before I ever wrote my first story, I began to understand the powerful influence of place—real and fictional—on my imagination.

When I was five, I decided to live on a ranch in Wyoming when I grew up. My passion for horses helps to explain the ranch part, but why Wyoming? Why not other ranching states, like Montana, or Texas? I credit media influence, specifically the Clint Walker movie *The Night of the Grizzly* and reruns of TV westerns such as *My Friend Flicka, The Virginian*, and *Laramie*, all set in Wyoming. For a little girl in a small North Carolina mountain town, Wyoming seemed pretty darned romantic, a mysterious western land. Even the shape of the name in my mouth—Why Ohm Eeng—felt exotic. In the front yard of my grandparents' Black Mountain mill village home, with the sound of Highway 70 traffic behind me, I'd set up my ranch under one of the twin oaks in the yard, using a tree trunk as a canyon wall, and play for hours with plastic horses and cows and split-rail fences sold in packs at the dime store, stopping occasionally to stare up through the tree limbs at the sky and dream.

After I learned to read, a little storybook called *Maria: Everybody Has a Name* by Dorothy Haas inspired an interest in New York City. Everything I knew about New York City came from *Family Affair*, a TV show about orphans living in a high-rise New York apartment with their uncle. That was how I recognized the setting in *Maria*, even though New York City is never mentioned in the story. But I knew it was the only place to find a girl named Maria, a man named Mr. Elefantopoulos, and a school within walking distance of a grocery store. The girls at my school had names like Tammy and June, and the nearest grocery store was at least five miles away. I was an adult before I noticed that the Shelby Café, where Mama always took my brother and me for lunch on back-to-school shopping days, was owned by a Greek family. All those years, in my very own town, there had been people with last names like Canoutas, Nicopoulos, and Psilopoulos.

When a Greek character with a love of cooking showed up while I was writing *The Big Beautiful*, I didn't have to wonder where he came from. "Cassandra could just hear Ruth Ann now, saying I told you so. She never did like the idea of Cassandra marrying Dennis, partly because of his mama's Greek side—foreigners, Ruth Ann called them, even though everyone had been born on American soil . . ."

Around age nine or ten, I discovered a new frontier when I read *Chris of Coorabeen* by M. A. O'Hanlon. From time to time my daddy would bring home boxes of discarded books from the nearby Kings Mountain or Belmont libraries, and that was where I found this treasure. On the inside cover of the book, written in my newly mastered, wobbly cursive, are these words: "This is a very good book. I highly recommend it!!" It's a wonderful novel about the adventures of a little girl and her two older brothers on their ranch in Australia. I was a little in love with Michael, the oldest brother, because his thoughtfulness reminded me of Jem in *To Kill a Mockingbird*. In *Moon Women*, I created for myself the protective older brother I'd always wanted: "A little while later, when Ruth Ann sat crying quietly in the corner, Dwight come in from helping his daddy with the milking. He was nearly grown then, and to Ruth Ann the sun rose and set in her brother. He didn't let the other boys pick on her, and he brung her candy when she was good."

That was also about the time I first read and fell in love with *Anne of Green Gables* by L. M. Montgomery. Prince Edward Island became another destination for my imagination, and I knew some day I'd see for myself places like Green Gables, and the White Way of Delight, and the Lake of Shining Waters. It turned out that Annie Laurie, an adolescent character in *The Big Beautiful*, loved this book too: "When it came to romance, Annie Laurie preferred Anne Shirley and Gilbert Blythe in *Anne of Green Gables*. But it would be hard to pick between Gilbert, and Jim in the Trixie Belden books. They were both so sweet."

When I was fifteen, my high school French Club spent a week in France. Oh, the excitement of riding an airplane for the first time, and eating snails, and taking the subway, and visiting the Eiffel Tower, Notre Dame, the Arc de Triomphe, the Louvre, the Rodin Museum, Napoleon's Tomb, and Chartres Cathedral. I was actually in a foreign country where people spoke a foreign language, the same country where my Pawpaw Price fought in World War I. The novelty was thrilling, but as much as I enjoyed the adventure, my overall impression of Paris was of a dirty city full of rude people. No matter how much I adored the language, France was filed away as a nice place to visit, but I wouldn't want to live there. In my short story "On the Inside Looking Out," the aftermath of an old soldier's experience in France echoes a looming violence: "Pappaw wears an American uniform. He's shell shocked and crazy as a loon. He sits over in his chair all day and talks to himself. He probably used to talk to Mama and Granny, but Granny's dead and Mama don't listen no more. I'll listen to him when I get the time, but it don't never make sense. There's a rat in my foxhole, he'll say, or my ears are full of blood and so are my boots, Captain."

In college, I longed to spend my junior year abroad in England, but lacked the courage to do anything about it. I finally made it to England in 1996 when the Girl Scout troop I worked with went to London for their senior trip. Highlights included the Tower of London, Big Ben, Westminster Abbey, St. Paul's Cathedral, and the street where Colin Firth's agent's office was located. It was the year after the miniseries based on *Pride and Prejudice* and starring Firth had aired in America; the agent's address was the closest thing to Colin I could find in an Internet search. An equally enamored friend and I waited across the street in the rain for nearly an hour, hoping to catch Colin going in or out (we didn't). Even so, England and Colin Firth changed my life. Until then, I'd never read Jane Austen, but after that trip I went on an Austen binge and added her to my list of literary heroes:

> What she wouldn't tell was that not only had she finished it, she'd reread the letter Captain Wentworth wrote Anne about ten times. Until she got to that part, she wasn't sure how she felt about the book, but that letter, oh boy, it about made her squeal, it was so romantic. "You pierce my soul," he said. "Tell me not that I am too late." It was almost as good as when Mr. Darcy tells Elizabeth Bennett, "You must allow me to tell you how ardently I admire and love you." (*The Big Beautiful*)

In my twenties I read mostly mainstream fiction and romances, until I discovered southern and Appalachian fiction, particularly stories set in North Carolina. Lee Smith, Wilma Dykeman, Doris Betts, Jill McCorkle, Clyde Edgerton, Robert Morgan, John Ehle, and on and on. It was a revelation. Literature did not take place only in New York City or Europe. Literature could and did happen right here in the Tar Heel State. With a sense of recognition and pride, I absorbed fiction that finally made me feel at home, especially fiction set in my native western North Carolina, like Wilma Dykeman's *The Tall Woman*:

There, standing with its hard firmness beneath her feet, her head and face bared to the wind that swept up from the deep valley below and broke in torrents against this ledge, she regained an inner quiet, a stillness she could not name or identify. It was as essential to her existence, however—had been even when she was still a child— as water or food itself. And as the wind struck her like a wave, taking her breath for the moment, beating and breaking against her, drowning her in an ocean of air, she was revived. And so she went back home, but returned to the rock again and again.

When I started writing my own fiction, it wasn't a deliberate, conscious decision to use North Carolina settings. Maybe because I'd heard the phrase "write what you know" so often, I automatically drew from familiar places: my grandparents' little red tar-paper house in Black Mountain; my parents' white brick suburban ranch-style home and the textile mill where they worked in Shelby; a cemetery in Walnut; a diner in Graham; a neighborhood, restaurant, and pier in Salter Path. The characters in my first novel, *Moon Women*, inhabited and were shaped by the same landscapes that produced my mother and maternal grandmother. Characters and setting were indistinguishable:

I remember finding her one day in the woods laying under this great big dogwood tree in full bloom. She was just a-laying there, not doing nothing but looking up through the limbs to the sky, and when I come up on her and said hey, she set up straight and I could see she'd been a-crying. I said, why, honey, what's the matter? and set down next to her, and she just shook her head and looked down at her hands. Then she looked back at me and said, oh, Mama, it's so beautiful I can't stand it, that's all. And she laid her head on my shoulder and cried some more, and then I set in to crying too.

With my second novel, *Plant Life*, I turned to the piedmont because I wanted to write about millworkers, people like my family, people who'd probably be working there still if not for NAFTA. Again, setting was inherent in the situation, a no-brainer: "Lottie May already worried too much about pink slips, ever since her daughters got laid off from the weave room last year. They all needed to forget the rumors about layoffs and the plant shutting down. That's all they was, anyhow, rumors, every year the same, and nothing ever come of them."

It was only while working on my third novel, *The Big Beautiful*, that I experienced a sense of conflict regarding the choice of setting. Only then did I come to realize how deeply and profoundly connected my writing is to my place. In the early stages of working on the novel, as I planned to write about a woman's midlife crisis, I had an epiphany. Or rather, the epiphany showed up in the form of a guy named Kevin who had come to North Carolina on a work trip and to visit mutual friends. He caught my interest first by being cute, but then, more importantly, because of where he was from. Prince Edward Island. Home of Anne Shirley. Home of L. M. Montgomery. Home of Gilbert Blythe. I got the brilliant idea to set part of my new novel in Prince Edward Island. I could take a research trip up there and visit Kevin. When a group of us went to supper at Cracker Barrel one night, I bombarded him with questions, excited to have a real live primary source in front of me. Then, a few days later, Kevin went home. My crush on him ended, but my crush on Prince Edward Island refused to die.

I immersed myself in research, spent hours in the library. Because I wanted to write about islands, the geographical as well as the human kind, and because my character loved the ocean, learning that the Micmac word for Prince Edward Island—*abegweit*—means "cradled in the waves" seemed like a sign that I was on the right path. It thrilled me to discover that Lucy Maud Montgomery once fell passionately in love with a farmer named Herman, a member of the family with

43

whom she boarded while teaching school, but he died tragically young before anything could come of it. And then to learn that she married a melancholy Presbyterian minister not for love but for protection, and because she didn't think she could do any better. Oh the drama! The heartbreak! The isolation! The long—and I mean very, very long—cold winters: "Here I am in the middle of the ocean, she thought, all by myself, not a human or a boat or a speck of land in sight, and I'm scared, but not near as scared as I ought to be. . . . She closed her eyes and felt herself drifting. What was that name Evelyn told her, the Indian name for Prince Edward Island. It was so beautiful. She couldn't think of it now, but it meant cradled on the waves." (*The Big Beautiful*)

But, as every writer knows, there comes that moment when you must step away from the research and begin to write. I left the library and began with my character cutting all ties to her home in North Carolina. She hopped on a bus bound for adventure in Canada and then . . . nothing. Nada. Dead end. The bus refused to leave the station. For weeks I fussed and fumed and fiddled, but it was no use. That novel wasn't going anywhere. It took a while before I finally realized that my character did not want to live on Prince Edward Island. She did not want to be Canadian. Her heart belonged to a place much closer to home.

> She needed to get to the edge of the land, to where she could breathe. She needed the ocean and sky, things so much bigger than her, she couldn't help but feel better standing next to them. She laid her head down on the top of the car, her arms spread wide, and closed her eyes, trying to picture the ocean the way it might look right now, all dark and mysterious, the white foam of the waves washing in and out, the lights of a shrimp boat on the water, the Cape Lookout light flashing way way off, maybe some heat lightning on the horizon. (*The Big Beautiful*)

Bogue Banks is an island in Carteret County, North Carolina, connected to the mainland by causeways at each end, one between Morehead City and Atlantic Beach and one between Cape Carteret and Emerald Isle. After nearly thirty years of vacationing there with my three best girlfriends, it feels like a second home, one that encompasses Emerald Isle, Atlantic Beach, Salter Path, Indian Beach, Fort Macon, Morehead City, Beaufort, Harkers Island, Cape Lookout, and Swansboro. Our vacations last only a week, sometimes two, never long enough. Until one of us wins the lottery, that's the way it has to be. But one of the wonderful things about writing is that you get to live vicariously through your characters. With my third novel, I decided my character and I would move to the beach. The island metaphor would still work, the setting would be a place I felt passionate about, and my character would experience a midlife crisis. The only difference was that now the story would unfold in a place where we both wanted to be, a place my senses knew from experience:

> The ocean made her feel lonesome too, but in a different way. The wind and waves and sky kept company with her, and something else too. It was the big mystery of it all, like a physical presence, that lay over the world, hushing it, making it be still. She felt like if she turned her head to just the right angle, she might hear something from the other side, like tuning in a radio signal from Canada or somewhere. It made her feel full, almost swelled up, the bigness of that mystery, the straining toward something she couldn't even name. . . . Cassandra flung her arms out, then laid back on the sand and closed her eyes. The wind blew across her body from the west, soft and warm. She could lay there all night, just let herself sink in the sand like that little mole crab, all warm and wet and safe. She looked up and saw the first star of the evening twinkling overhead and closed her eyes again.
> (*The Big Beautiful*)

In order to write about the place with as much of an insider's perspective as possible, I returned to the library, read everything I could find, subscribed to the *Carteret County News-Times*, called up strangers at the Coast Guard and asked them things like, "How long can you be out in the ocean alone before you drown or get eaten by something?" (Not long.) And, "What do you call the ropey thing they throw over the side of a boat so people can climb up and get in?" (Cargo net.) As I learned about the people, the culture, the lifestyles, the economy, the weather, and a million other details, my relationship with the place became much more intense, the way I imagine a long friendship might turn suddenly into a romance.

This time when I stepped away from the research and sat down to write, when I changed direction and headed east instead of north, the novel's engine finally roared to life. I got rid of the bus, put my character in a limousine headed for the North Carolina coast, and never looked back:

> Highway 58 sliced the island in two, dividing the sound side from the ocean side. They were almost like two different worlds. The houses on the ocean side sat huge and exposed to whatever blew in off the ocean. The houses on the sound side, tucked in among live oaks and beach hills, were smaller, not as fancy. . . . It was tough maneuvering the big limo on the narrow sandy lanes. . . . She remembered the house being white, but now it was painted bright blue and seemed to blend in with the sky and sound behind it. At the open living room windows, white lace curtains fluttered against the screens, and out back a long line of men's shirts and pants flapped in the breeze. Past the clothesline, two boats—one little and one big—bumped against the dock and past that, white caps rose and fell in the choppy waters of the sound. Enough, she thought. Enough like home, and enough different.
> (*The Big Beautiful*)

My infatuations with far-off places never presented any real competition for the deep and abiding devotion I have always felt for my first place, my home place, North Carolina. This devotion is why something in me lights up when I find books with a North Carolina connection. It's why I always cry at the end of the 1974 film *Where the Lilies Bloom*, which was filmed in Watauga County, and during the opening credits of the 1992 film *The Last of the Mohicans*, also filmed in western North Carolina. The sense of recognition and pride I feel seeing my home state on the page or screen makes me feel silly and sappy, but I can't help it. That pride is why I cram the names of as many of my homes as I can into my author bio: Swannanoa, Black Mountain, Shelby, Chapel Hill, Saxapahaw, Graham, Cullowhee, Webster. It's why I've never doubted that North Carolina truly is a vale of humility between two mountains of conceit. It's why, when I cross back into North Carolina on my way home from another state, I whoop and holler as if I've just won the lottery. And I reckon, in a way, I have.

Sharon McCrumb puts it this way in "The First Appalachian Journey":

Perhaps it isn't a unique experience in nature, this yearning for a place to which one is somehow connected. After years in the vast ocean, salmon return to spawn in the same small stream from whence they and their forbears came; monarch butterflies make the journey from the eastern seaboard to the same field in Mexico that had been the birthplace of the previous generation. The journey there and back again is unchanging, but each generation travels only one way. Is it really so strange that humans might feel some of this magnetism toward the land itself?

Relief

MICHAEL MCFEE

1.

In late August 1986, I was a Tar Heel in exile, and happy about it. I'd just begun my year as poet-in-residence at Cornell, I had a spacious apartment in an old house near campus, and I had time to write every day, a luxury not enjoyed at home in North Carolina. What more could a young poet ask?

The first week in Ithaca was wonderfully productive, a literary dream. The second week was less satisfying, because I'd begun to miss my wife and two-year-old son, nine hours to the south: she would take a leave from her job in January so that they could come live with me during the wintry "spring" semester, but till then the two of them had to stay back in Durham. The third week was terrible: I missed them so much I couldn't really concentrate on any work. All I did was count the days and hours and minutes till I saw them in the Syracuse airport.

When my little boy came toddling down the ramp from the gates, I called his name and ran toward him and then (much to my surprise) collapsed. My legs gave way. I sank to the dirty tiles. I started crying. I was tearfully overjoyed to see him, to hear and touch and smell him, simply to *be* with him and his mother, my wife, the loves of my life. I had been physically craving their presence, and now the distance was closed—for a few days, at least.

To a less-dramatic degree, yet in the same way, that's how I feel about my native place, western North Carolina, in particular south Buncombe County and Asheville and the surrounding terrain. I've lived a full and fortunate life in the piedmont, 225 miles to the east, for over four decades, but I've never stopped missing the mountains, longing for them, yearning to return for a little while. I need to migrate there, now and then. My body seems to require elevation, the kind of serious geographical relief you can't get in Durham County, where I live, or Orange County, where I work. No matter how many times I've driven I-40 West, when I get the first clear view of those imbricate blue ranges unfolding ahead of me, at the Dysartville Road exit between Morganton and Marion, my eyes tear up, my pulse quickens, and I fall silent in gratitude. I feel *relieved*. I'm home.

2.

It was not always thus.

I couldn't wait to escape the mountains, once I approached college age. My childhood and teenhood there were pretty happy, all in all, but I never considered attending an upland university. I wanted to be in a bigger, busier, more worldly place, one not isolated by encircling hills.

Maybe reading *Look Homeward, Angel* at the hormone-addled age of sixteen (perfect timing) planted this seed, or helped water it. But by the time I headed to the School of Design at N.C. State, I was ready to put the mountains behind me.

3.

I could put the mountains behind me, in the rearview mirror, but I hadn't grasped an unexpected physiological fact: they were somehow *inside* me, deep in my body and mind.

Once in Raleigh, I found myself looking for hills at the horizon, behind all those brick buildings: not there. I found myself listening to the way people talked, and wishing I could hear the pointed Appalachian locutions of my family. (Not that I would have known to call them "Appalachian" at that time; such regional self-consciousness was not part of my education in Buncombe County Schools.) I found myself craving the switchback of a mountain road, the steep climb and fall of a trail, the changes in feet above sea level that I'd taken for granted. As a pithy fellow hillbilly once said while sojourning in the piedmont: "Ain't enough vertical element to this."

After I transferred to Chapel Hill in 1974, and signed up for a creative writing class, and got over Trying To Sound Like an English Poet in my poems, and discovered contemporary western North Carolina writers, I found myself going back to the mountains I couldn't put behind me after all, in lines and stanzas, in poem after poem, in elegies for what I'd left behind but still loved. I felt like I gained strength from touching that higher ground, if only in words.

4.

For fun, sometime toward the end of elementary school—grades one through eight, at old Valley Springs School in Skyland, which housed all twelve grades when I started there—I wrote out my complete address:

Mike McFee
160 Locust Court
Royal Pines
Arden
Buncombe County
North Carolina
United States of America
North America
Western Hemisphere
Earth

As the teacher's pet and class egghead, I probably wanted to elaborate on the astronomical location, but I stopped with Earth, fortunately. What did I know, really, about space, or (for that matter) the globe, or the wide-flung country and state? What I did know was the first four lines in that strung-out list: our house, our neighborhood, our town, our county. What I knew—what rooted and nourished me then, and later as a writer—was the local: it was my world, if not *the* world, and those places anchored me.

5.

Locust Court was one of several dozen streets in Royal Pines, a lower-middle-class subdivision clumped along Highways 25 and 25A, midway between Asheville and Hendersonville. Most of the streets were named for trees. Locust was between Walnut and Chestnut: it began at Cedar Lane then climbed (over several long hills—we lived at the top of the first one) across Royal Pines Drive and past Hemlock Street, ending at Oak Terrace and Hickory Court, its terminus pointed toward the 2,996-foot summit of Mount Royal. This may sound rather sylvan and poetic, but in fact most of the houses were small and cheaply made, and most of the families were, like us, working-class at best. There was nothing particularly distinctive about Royal Pines, no upscale sidewalks or streetlights or "improvements": it was just streets and lots and people getting by.

Which made it a great place to be a kid. From an early age, I could, and did, simply *roam*. On foot, on bike, by myself or with my dog, I'd visit friends' houses, I'd look for a pickup game to join, and I'd explore the vacant lots or undeveloped woods. I'd head out the door and be gone all day, and—in that earlier, safer, less paranoid time—nobody worried about it. I waged hot dirt-clod and crabapple wars with my buddies, I played kick the can at dusk with the kissable girls; I used my imagination and my wits and, once or twice, my fists.

The adults could be pretty interesting. One neighbor was a shell-shocked WWII veteran who would utter wildly inappropriate profanities or sexual remarks, then immediately forget them. One was a hard-living woman whose sons loved

Richard Petty more than God, and kept a blue #43 Plymouth in the yard. One was a genteel man from Florida who lived with his Cadillac-driving ancient mother; after their boxer dogs attacked and disfigured the next-door-neighbor girl, he destroyed them and we rarely saw him outside again.

Have I written about all this? You bet. Locust Court gave me place, images, character, story, *relief.* There was nothing flat about the place, metaphorically or literally: you were always going up or down, even walking to the mailbox or your beat-up car. The street I lived on has a cameo in the first poem in my mercifully out-of-print first book, which offers "Directions" to an idealized location in the mountains: "the sunken asphalt / patch that looks like Africa" was right in front of our house, one of many ineffectual repairs on the cracked concrete streets of Royal Pines.

6.

There was nothing regal about the Royal Pines of my youth, and many of the tall evergreens had been cut down. (My sarcastic best friend said it should be called Royal Stumps.) I was painfully aware of how much less grand it was than, say, Oak Forest, an affluent development close to the high school where all the cutest girls and coolest guys seemed to live, in huge brick houses with finished basements and lush green yards.

But that was not the original plan for our neighborhood.

A two-page spread in the *Asheville Times* of Sunday, May 31, 1925, announced "the Formal Opening of Beautiful Royal Pines," whose handsome logo—a stylized pine flanked by a capital *R* and *P*, set inside a crown—proclaimed it "Asheville's Suburb Supreme." "Thursday," the ad proclaimed, "on the Dixie Highway, between the resort cities of Asheville and Hendersonville, Royal Pines will be the scene of unusual interest as thousands will be introduced to the Many Wonderful Features of this Superb Estate which has been in the process of development for nearly 100 years and is positively peerless in its Rare Beauty." Across the tops of the pages were "A Photographic Reproduction of the Beautiful Painting, 8 x 20 feet, executed by L. Francis—the largest in North Carolina—portraying Asheville, Kenilworth, Biltmore, and Royal Pines," and an "Interesting Drawing Showing the Location of Royal Pines with Relation to Asheville and Other Points on the Dixie Highway," including the Biltmore House and the Biltmore Forest Country Club and Golf Course.

Which is to say: the developer of Royal Pines, the William I. Phillips Company, was aiming pretty high, or at least associating this new development with the classier parts of Asheville. "Here, on a delightful elevation of 2,300 to 2,600 feet, with a magnificent view of Mt. Pisgah and several mountain ranges, will be erected many fine homes, since practically every lot is amply large enough to permit the building of a pretentious home." All this overheated copy—with its pretentious use of "pretentious" and Important Capital Letters—was intended not for western North Carolinians but for rich folks from Florida or New York, looking to invest their money in a summer home, a scaled-down version of George Vanderbilt's chateau but "fine" nonetheless. There was even going to be a Royal Pines Casino, "a magnificent structure—with a large swimming pool, a dance floor, locker room, and a grandstand—destined to be the center of Asheville's social life throughout the entire summer season." Suburb supreme, indeed!

What went wrong? Despite the real estate hype, most lots were barely half an acre, puny by the standards of Biltmore Forest, the genuinely posh suburb that Vanderbilt's widow, Cornelia, began developing on estate land earlier in the 1920s. Royal Pines was hardly a century old or "peerless in its Rare Beauty": its residents did not enjoy "magnificent mountain views," much less the promised "planted parkways" and other "high-class development" amenities.

But the real problem was the stock-market crash of 1929 three years later, when Royal Pines was still struggling to get off the ground. Nobody had money to invest, and the suburb never really got developed in a supreme manner, despite the alliterative effort. When lots and houses finally did get sold—like, say, Lot 16 on Block 16, a.k.a. 160 Locust Court, in August 1947—the purchasers were not wealthy Miamians looking for a seasonal cottage, but hardscrabble locals like my just-married parents buying a small house and lot they could make into a respectable suburban place over the coming decades.

Did I know any of this local history, growing up? No. And my folks didn't tell me, if they knew. But in the layout of the streets, in a few of the original houses, in the very name itself, Royal Pines, there was always the hint of something grander having almost happened there. Which is the sweet spot for a writer.

7.

Arden, the next ring on my elementary address bulls-eye, didn't exactly exist. As the *North Carolina Gazetteer* drolly notes: "Incorporated 1883, but long inactive in municipal affairs." Unlike Biltmore Forest, there was no town, no town hall, no sense of Arden as a civic unit. It was a not-so-wide place on the road near Henderson County: when I was growing up, if you drove less than a mile in any direction, there was nothing but deep darkness and stars out there.

The *Gazetteer* continues: "Known first as Shufordsville. Renamed Arden for the Forest of Arden in Shakespeare's *As You Like It*." As with Royal Pines, the name Arden embodied higher aspirations: rather than simply name your place for the most prolific clan in the area, why not go for something finer, exclusive sounding, dramatically sylvan? And as with Royal Pines, the reality fell short of the dream.

The *Gazetteer* concludes: "Alt. 2,225." The elevation at our Locust Court address, according to the Buncombe County Online Slope Calculation Tool, is 2,340 feet, roughly 2,000 feet higher than the house where I now live in Durham. I grew up at elevation. Life there always involved verticality, going higher or lower, not merely continuing out and out and out, as in the flatlands. Though I couldn't see Pisgah's peak (alt. 5,271) from my yard, it was looming at the horizon, waiting for me to come to a clearing and spy it in the distance, crowning the ridge to the southwest, one of many dozens of mountains whose blue relief was a carved border always grounding the sky.

8.

Asheville itself wasn't part of my youthful address, because I didn't actually reside there; but it was, and is, very much a part of my life.

Granny McFee lived—with various female kin: all the men were departed—at 76 Arlington, a few blocks off Charlotte Street, at the other end of that thoroughfare from the hightone Grove Park Inn neighborhood. Hers was a skinny clapboard house with a second floor (intriguing to me: no upper stories in Royal Pines) and a root cellar under the side porch, a spooky pit where she kept her many canned goods. I can close my eyes and still see every room. When I opened the front door, vivid smells greeted me, mostly from her cooking—my grandmother's Thanksgiving meal was truly a heavenly feast—but also from her arthritis and asthma remedies. She and her sisters and daughters doted on me, and I did not resist. I was not allowed to roam, since Asheville was the Big City and therefore dangerous, but if they'd let me, I would've gone out the front door and turned right, up the steep hill, and tromped onto Beaucatcher Mountain (alt. 3,200), just as I wandered around Mount Royal out in the county.

Asheville offered urban pleasures, though. My mother took my sister and me to Pack Memorial Library, back when it was actually on Pack Square. How exotic, the child-scale wooden Indian inside the entrance! How exciting, being allowed to touch and read and check out so many books! She also took us to the S&W Cafeteria on Patton Avenue, that stylish Deco building: how adult I felt there, eating my cherry pie, fetching fresh coffee for Mom as she smoked her after-dinner cigarette. And she hauled us into town to attend First Baptist Church, that elegant domed place of worship. We could've gone to Arden Baptist Church, not a mile from our house in Royal Pines, but Mom—a social dreamer if not an actual social climber, who adored the Biltmore House and First Baptist and the S&W, monuments to loftier cultural possibilities—wanted us to worship with the most refined Baptists in the area.

Have I written about all this? Oh yes. The Asheville that I knew growing up—where my beloved grandmother and aunts lived, where we ate out and bought clothes, where we went to church and the library and the movies—is not the groovy Asheville of today, with its hipsters and wealthy retirees and lively beer-and-food culture. Back then, the new mall was draining downtown of its businesses, and the still-mired-in-Depression-debt city had a somewhat abandoned feel. But I loved going there, and simply walking its hilly blocks, and still do. It's personal: there's the old post office where my father worked the graveyard shift, there's the Grove Arcade where my mother processed foreign meteorological data for the government, there's Bon Marché department store where several aunts were salesladies, there's Tops for Shoes where my sister and I got our feet x-rayed, there's the Flatiron Building where we went to the dentist. And there's where I—a naïve seventeen-year-old would-be literary scholar, preparing to write his senior thesis on James Joyce—bought a copy of *Ulysses* at Talman's: the wry bookseller, a tall man, looked down at me over his glasses and said, "You think you're ready for this, pal?"

9.

imes when I'm back in Asheville, I'll visit my parents.
buried in the Rest Haven section of Green Hill Cem-

etery west of downtown, across the French Broad River, off busy Patton Avenue. Mom and Dad are side by side, near the topmost point in the graveyard, with a fine view of Mount Pisgah to the southwest on a clear day. I'll clean off their flat stones, maybe put some nice artificial flowers in the sunken pots, and give them the most recent family news.

From 1958 to 1962, they bought four plots on the installment plan: one for each of them, one for their daughter, and one for their son. My estranged sister died in 2006 at the age of fifty-four, and her ashes were scattered somewhere along the Blue Ridge Parkway by her companion of many years—I don't know where. Her space will never be used, not by her. Though I like the idea of enjoying a prospect of Pisgah for eternity, I won't use the space waiting for me, either: my own family and homeplace are elsewhere now. I think I'll leave that plot, that narrow little lot, undeveloped.

10.

My knowledge of Buncombe County, the last local item in my address list, was selective. Mostly, it was focused on and around the Parkway, that most sublime of tourist roads, looping into Buncombe County from the northeast, curving past Craggy Gardens and down toward Asheville but then swooping south of the city, between it and Arden, before climbing back up into the national forest to Mount Pisgah and the Haywood County line. That's a lot of picturesque blacktop, and my family liked to take Sunday afternoon drives along the Parkway: it was, or at least felt like, free entertainment when gas was thirty cents a gallon or less, gliding on that two-lane highway above the valley where we spent the rest of the week, looking down on the world and out at the sweet bluegreen view, passing through tunnels and sometimes disappearing into fog or clouds but always emerging on the other side, in the clear, nearly a mile high in the sky.

Such prospects, such perspective, stirred the young poet in

me. In fact, the first poem in my senior creative writing thesis at UNC, called "Overlook," was about pulling off the Parkway and savoring the view. But that came years later. When I was a teenager, especially once I learned to drive, the Blue Ridge Parkway was about two things.

One was romance. I liked to take prospective girlfriends on a nice long ride up that road whose mountain prospects rendered conversation unnecessary, parking the car at a remote overlook, then hiking to a more secluded spot where we could recline on a blanket and enjoy a picnic and, I hoped, each other. There was something about canoodling in the open air, at 4,000 feet, that felt practically Edenic, the two of us isolated in a high green garden with a long blue view, flushed and happy.

But such occasions were, believe me, rare. Mostly, the Parkway was about hiking and camping, on my own or with friends. Many remarkable trails began at or crossed over that road, and I took lots of them across ridges, up to peaks, down to secluded valleys: those walks were excellent lessons in staying alert, in using every sense to experience the world around me as carefully and fully as possible. Sometimes, a friend and I would hike deeper into the national forest, pitch our tent by a creek or river, cook up dinner over a Coleman stove, and sleep out in the woods with the other animals. I'll never forget waking one March morning, near John Rock, to absolute silence and stillness, and a canvas roof sagging inches from my face: out of nowhere, it had snowed several feet overnight. For hours, we made our weighty way through holy dazzle back to the car, without seeing or hearing another human being. It was glorious.

11.

Did growing up in the mountains predispose me to be a poet?

Probably not. And yet, the daily vertical movement of living at higher altitudes is not unlike the experience of writing a poem, which doesn't so much cross the page as descend it, in a kind of back-and-forth dance. The turn at the end of each line is not unlike the turn at a switchback, reversing to where you came from but a bit lower, making progress toward a desired but unpredictable destination, your load lightening somehow. Paying close attention on steep trails and roads is not unlike stepping deliberately along the poetic line, sustaining your rhythm and momentum just so, not too fast but not too slow, focusing on the details underfoot and at hand while also appreciating the long view, if you lift your eyes to the horizon.

Of course, "not unlike" is not "like." And yet, it's close. It's kin.

12.

Hanging on the wall in my home office:

1. A sixteen-by-twenty-one-inch black-and-white print, *1891. Bird's-Eye View of the City of Asheville, North Carolina*—a reproduction of the original, issued by Bon Marché department store in August 1947, the month my parents married and bought the Royal Pines property. The little county seat ("Population 1880, 2,610; 1890, 11,500") looks like a wilderness town, with the forest creeping in from the west, and with not that many buildings clustered on its streets— the 1876 courthouse on the square, the churches on Church Street, and the original Battery Park Hotel on Haywood, from whose porch George Vanderbilt first saw Pisgah, twenty miles away to the south, a mountain he would later own, as well as all the valley between him and that peak. Most of the named structures on this View are long gone, e.g., the huge Asheville Furniture Manufactory by the flood-prone French Broad, running along the bottom of the print; but what's still there is the landscape, the underlying topography, the bones which the modern city's flesh covers: the flats by the river, "Vally" Street (the African American part of town) clearly in a valley below Market Street hill, the shadow-casting ridges rising up

and climbing to the north/south path of Main Street, the undeveloped acclivity of Beaucatcher disappearing beyond the
top of the print. Arlington Street is not labeled, but I see the
beginning of its first block, and—with my magnifying glass—I
can guess where my grandmother's house will soon be built,
where my father's family will situate itself, near the foot of
that in-town mountain.

2. A Transverse Mercator Projection of the Knoxville
quadrant (NI 17-1) of the U.S. Geological Survey—which is
to say, a twenty-by-thirty-one-inch plastic representation of
the mountains from Marion, North Carolina, to east Tennes-
see, the elevation contours rendered in 3-D relief, so that the
scale-model ridges and peaks rise up like actual ridges and
peaks from the plain of the sheet. Unlike the 1891 Bird's-Eye
View, which is after all a fanciful elaboration of a city map,
filled out with nonexistent individual trees and generic structures, this Mercator Projection NI 17-1 bristles with accurate
data, as you might expect from something prepared by the
Defense Mapping Agency Topographic Center: numbered
roads, named towns and bodies of water and mountains,
railroads and county lines, longitude and latitude. Asheville
is a sprawling yellow blob in the valley interrupting Pisgah
National Forest, and Royal Pines is a speck on the Skyland/
Arden drip from that blob.

This map has brought me many hours of pleasure. I can
study it on the wall, running my fingers along the crest-
hugging Blue Ridge Parkway, touching the top of Mount
Royal in Arden, following the flow of the Davidson River
past John Rock. I can find unmarked Max Patch (4,629 feet),
where my mother spent the war handling accounts at a lumber mill, way out in the wild Great Smoky Mountains on the
N.C./Tenn. state line. I can lay the projection flat on a table,
and kneel till my eye is at map level, or I can lay it on the
floor and look down as if from a great height: either way, the
rumpled complicated landscape of home is there, spread out
before or below me, and for a few seconds—squinting—I can

pretend that I'm actually seeing it. That cartographic comfort has helped me through some cold homesick times in Ithaca, in Appleton, and even in Durham, when my eyes and heart and imagination needed a little relief.

13.

The first poem in my first book was set in the mountains, and so is the last poem in my most recent book, a twenty-seven-part sequence called "McCormick Field," set in and around the baseball park in Asheville where my father and I spent our closest times together.

Mountainous poems frame my poetry-publishing career, so far. That made me wonder: how many of the poems in my books are actually set in Buncombe County or western North Carolina, or deal with family characters and stories from there, or somehow involve that Appalachian part of the world?

The tally:

My seven full-length "regular" poetry collections contain 223 poems total. Of those, 116 deal with mountain material, in whole or in part.

In particular: 10 of the 30 poems in my first book had to do with the mountains; 19 of 23 in the second; 22 of 22 in the third, wholly based on the life of my Appalachian mother; and then, 13 of 41, 18 of 39, 17 of 37, and 17 of 31.

At first, I was shocked at those high percentages, especially since I haven't lived in the Blue Ridge for over forty years. But the more I thought about it, the less I was surprised: "When I need inspiration," as I said in an interview years ago, "I automatically go back to the mountains in my writing." They seem to be my given subject matter, my default mode as a writer. Living at a distance from the hills seems to provide a helpful clarifying perspective, and sharpens the yearning to return in poems and essays.

And I don't seem to be done yet. One of the books I've been

working on for a while is about the early years of Biltmore, from 1888—when Vanderbilt conceived the idea of buying land south of Asheville and building a grand chateau, the biggest private home in America—into the very early twentieth century. What got me going on this project was wondering: what happened to the mountain people who were actually living on those hundreds of thousands of acres that the richest bachelor in the world bought? What effect did that millionaire's ambition have on the locals, in one of the poorest corners of the country? Were any ancestral McFees displaced by the Vanderbilts?

One day I may stop mining the mountain vein. But I doubt it. I don't think I want to. I don't think I can.

The Piedmont

Salad Days

LEE SMITH

MAY 1965

We leave Hollins at 10:00 A.M., six of us crammed into the car, Mary Withers driving.

"My Girl" is on the radio. Some of us know our dates; some don't. I don't. He is an SAE, but I can't remember his name. I am already tired. I have been up for hours, ironing my clothes, ironing my hair. At Martinsville, we stop for gas and road beer. We sing along with the radio. Now it's "Help Me Rhonda" by the Beach Boys. We are getting real hot in the car because it doesn't have any air conditioning, but we can't open the windows much because we would mess up our hair. I keep trying to remember my date's name. We stop in Danville for more road beer. "Ticket to Ride" is on the radio. Now we are in Chapel Hill; now we are pulling up in front of the fraternity house; now all these boys are standing up and walking out to the car. Oh no. What is his name? Oh no.

Later, that same night, in formal clothes, we walk right up the middle of Franklin Street, giggling and singing. Doug Clark and the Hot Nuts played at the party. My date passed out, but now I have another date. He is from Scotland Neck, which I find hysterically funny. The sun is coming up. I'm carrying my shoes. It was some party.

Portions of this narrative were adapted from "Blue Heaven: A Chapel Hill Memory Album," which appeared in *Close to Home: Revelations and Reminiscences of North Carolina Authors*, edited by Lee Harrison Child (Winston-Salem, N.C.: John F. Blair, Publisher, 1996).

JUNE 1966

Summer School. I sit on the grass near the Davie Poplar, books thrown down beside me. A soft wind blows my hair. I stretch out my legs. The boy puts his head on my lap. He wears a pastel knit shirt, pastel slacks, loafers. He looks like an Easter egg. But he is a golfer. I sigh languidly. I am in love.

AUGUST 1966

It is a hot, smoky café, the smoke barely stirred by the sluggish overhead fan. The backs of my legs stick to the sticky wooden booth. This conversation is the most intense conversation I have ever had, and also the most beer I have ever drunk. It is very, very late. This is a great conversation, I can't believe how significant it is. He leans across the table toward me. He pounds on the table to make a point. With his other hand, he touches my knee under the table. He is a member of the SDS. We light more cigarettes. I am in love.

AUGUST 1967

It is raining, and we have been walking for hours, in a light, fine drizzle that jewels the edges of everything. We are soaked through. We stop to sit on one of the gray stone walls that are everywhere in Chapel Hill. We kiss. I run my finger along the jeweled stone. This time I am really in love. Later, much later, he will move to Chicago, taking my life-size painting of the Supremes and breaking my heart. Eventually I will recover. He was from Connecticut and talked funny.

JUNE 1973

Finally, I move to Chapel Hill with my husband, James Seay, a poet who has gotten a job teaching at UNC. I have always wanted to live here. So has everybody else who ever went to school here, and once school is over, many of them can't stand to leave. So everybody who comes to work on our house has a Ph.D. in something: the plumber's degree is in philosophy; the painter is a historian. I am embarrassed to have all these educated people doing manual labor on my house. I offer them coffee and cake. The carpenter listens to opera while he builds bookshelves. I have second thoughts—are we cool enough to live in Chapel Hill? I won't let the children play with toy guns while the workmen are here, so they won't think we are rednecks.

SEPTEMBER 1973

It is the first day of my new job teaching language arts at Carolina Friends School. I got this job by telephone from Nashville, where I'd been teaching seventh grade at Harpeth Hall, a prestigious girls' school. There the girls wore green and gold uniforms, the school colors, and the faculty dressed up. So I'm all ready for my first day at Carolina Friends, wearing a red linen suit with a straight skirt, pearls, patent-leather heels, and stockings.

Only, I can't find the school. I drive out into the countryside as directed, on narrow roads past fields and cows and split-rail fences, and then finally turn onto an unpaved road which disappears ahead of me into the forest. This can't be right! Gradually I perceive a number of ramshackle buildings here and there in the trees, then a large log house, apparently built by hand, up the hill, with a sizable deck running all around it. Built by hand? Where's the school? Harpeth Hall had a stone wall around its landscaped grounds, with paved walkways running everywhere.

Finally I spot an old man in a baseball cap and overalls, trudging up the road carrying a toolbox. I pull beside him and announce, "I'm looking for Carolina Friends School."

"Well, you've found us." He gives me a big smile and sticks

his hand in the window for me to shake. I had him pegged as a janitor, but maybe not.

"But where are the students?" I still haven't seen one.

He points up the hill at the log house.

"They're settling in," he says.

I stare at him.

"We start every day with meditation," he says. "Quiet time."

Really? I'm still thinking as I park in a cluster of old pickups and vans with peace signs on them. I have never known any middle school students to be capable of quiet time, much less meditation. It's pretty hard walking up the pebbly dirt road in these patent-leather heels, covered by dust when I finally make it.

Nobody seems to be around, so I go on in the open door, mortified to find myself suddenly in the midst of about seventy people, young and old, all of them down on the polished wood floor where they form a huge ragged circle in every posture imaginable, heads mostly bowed, eyes mostly closed. Everybody's wearing blue jeans, cutoffs, or shorts, with sneakers, flip-flops—or simply bare feet. There's a giant, colorful, hand-woven mandala on the wall above them. Across the big room I spot a guy I somehow know to be Don Wells, the head of the school, the guy who hired me on the phone. He's got long, blondish hair, he's sitting cross-legged, grinning at me. He does not get up. Out of some wrongheaded perversity I pick my way through the meditating students and then across the open part of the circle, my heels clicking on the shining wood floor. Nobody says a word. Only, when I have almost made it, here comes a long, single, expert wolf whistle, and then a rising chorus of other wolf whistles. Oh no. I feel myself turning as red as this smart little red suit which I will never, ever, wear again. The guy Don gets up and hugs me, laughing. Now everybody is laughing, scrambling to their feet, heading outdoors. Another teacher brings me some sandals so I can go out and participate in the ropes course and the relay races and the trust-building exercises . . . well, some of them, anyway.

I'm getting the drill—or the lack of the drill, I should say. Apparently they have no uniforms and no school colors and no sports except for Ultimate Frisbee, whatever that is. I stand out on the deck looking down at the hilly, wooded landscape covered with kids and grown-ups in all kinds of activities which are, I realize suddenly, much less random than they seem. This will turn out to be true of everything.

I am surprised and horrified to hear my first assignment, which is to plan and buy the food for 100 people for one day of our upcoming weekend retreat at Quaker Lake.

"I don't know anything about feeding that many people. I just can't do that," I tell Don.

"Oh, sure you can," Don says.

At my first faculty meeting that afternoon, I have to settle in, too. Then Don welcomes me and asks, "What individual courses do you want to teach?"

"Well, what are the requirements?" I ask. "I mean, the curriculum."

"We're in the process of figuring that out," Don says. "You tell me."

Everybody speaks up. They all listen to each other. They all have great ideas. I have no ideas. In fact, I'm having a panic attack, but then something else starts happening. Somewhere, way down inside, it's like a dam gives way and I start getting excited. I love plays. I have always wanted kids to write plays and then put them on. I have always wanted to teach a class that mixes up art and writing . . . or photography and writing. . . . I have always wanted to teach ghost stories, and Greek mythology, and poetry out loud, really loud. Also I've got this recipe for taco pie casserole which might work great for that retreat . . .

SUMMER, MID-1970S

A party on Stinson Street, probably Anne Jones's house. Everybody I know has lived on Stinson Street at one time or another. Stinson Street has constant parties, constant yard sales. Anyway, at some point during one of these parties, I go outside to get some air and wander across the street to Leonard Rogoff's yard sale, where I stand transfixed before a chest of drawers with a mirror attached to the top of it. I stand before the chest and look into the mirror for a long time. The mirror is tilted so that I can see a tree, the moon, my face. Oh no, I think. This is really my life, and I am really living it. I remember thinking that then, on Stinson Street.

LATE '70S, EARLY '80S

I sit on the edge of the Rainbow Soccer Field, where my kids are playing Rainbow Soccer, which is noncompetitive. You can't yell anything like "Kill 'em!" or "Stomp 'em!" This is hard for some parents. My son Josh is playing center forward. I am writing a novel.

I sit at the Chapel Hill Tennis Club, waiting for my son's match to start. This is my son Page. He's real good. I am writing a novel.

I sit on a wing chair before the fire in the Chapel Hill Public Library on Franklin Street . . . in a booth at Breadmen's . . . at a picnic table at University Lake . . . on a quilt at Umstead Park . . . in a wicker chair on my own back porch on Burlage Circle. I am writing a novel. I am always writing a novel in this town. Nobody cares. Nobody bugs me. Nobody thinks a thing about it. Everybody else is writing a novel, too.

"In Chapel Hill, throw a rock and you'll hit a writer," someone once said. This has always been true. For Chapel Hill is primarily a town of the mind, a town of trees and visions. Thomas Wolfe praised the "rare romantic quality of the atmosphere." Maybe the quiet, leafy streets themselves are still informed by his giant spirit, that wild young man from the mountains who raged through them in his archetypal search for identity.

The much-loved English professor Hugh Holman wrote,

"The primary thing that Chapel Hill gives those who come to be a part of it is the freedom to be themselves. It is an unorganized town. It is easy to persuade its citizens, along with the students of the university, to join briefly in a cause, to march for a little while beneath a banner . . . but to remain permanently organized is something else indeed, for Chapel Hill does not organize very well. Those who come to this town can find in it just about the quantity of freedom to be themselves which they wish to have."

CIRCA 1980

I am with my children, and we run into some of their friends from their former community church preschool, along with the friends' mother.

"Hello, Naomi," I say. "Hi, Johnny."

"We have changed our names," their mother says. "This is Trumpet Vine"—she indicates Naomi—"and this is Golden Sun. I myself am Flamingo."

Oh my, I think. Oh no. My kids do not think that Trumpet Vine is a very good name. But then my younger son, Page, changes his own name (briefly) to Rick. He has always hated Page, a family name; he gets teased because it is too girly. Soon after this, Trumpet Vine, Golden Sun, and Flamingo moved away from Chapel Hill with some kind of sect. I think they were called the Orange People.

I never changed my name, but I have thought about it ever since. I would go with three syllables, too: Biloxi, Chardonnay, Sunflower . . .

SURPRISES, SPRING 1981

. . . though in retrospect, it seems inevitable. Both people of good will, my husband and I have been kept together by children and family and friends and common interests, but we are very different. When he suddenly moves out, I am traumatized. I am thirty-seven, old as the hills, old as dirt. And now I am getting a divorce. My mother bursts into tears. "Nobody in our family has EVAH gotten a divorce," she weeps, though later she will admit that a numbah of them should have. My mountain father weighs in with his mountain advice: "Change the locks and get a handgun." I don't do that. I do lose twenty pounds, almost overnight. In fact, I lose everything, leaving jackets and purses all over town. I let my boys ride their skateboards through our empty house and eat exclusively from the Red Food Group so beloved by boys (Spaghettios, Hawaiian Punch, bacon, barbecued potato chips). I take them skiing in Colorado with my cousins for Spring Break.

I desperately need a real job instead of the part-time position I've got. Suddenly one comes up at N.C. State University, full-time. Only I don't have the nerve to apply for it, I don't have the academic credentials. "Don't give me that crap," Doris Betts says. "Just go for it." She pushes me into it, and to my surprise I get the job, which I will keep for nineteen years.

On Valentine's Day I get myself together as my mother used to say, and go out for an afternoon Valentine Party thrown by Marilyn Hartman who directs the Evening College at Duke University, where I teach creative writing once a week. Here I meet another writer, a journalist named Hal Crowther, a recent transplant from Buffalo who is teaching critical writing in this same program. I know who he is, I have been admiring his columns in the new *Spectator* magazine. We start talking and it turns out that we have both stashed our children in video parlors so we can come to this party. Then we start talking about Robert Stone's recent novel, *A Flag for Sunrise*, which we have both just read. Hal keeps rattling his tiny cup in his tiny saucer and looking for wine. But there's only tea. "Would you like to go out for a drink sometime?" he asks.

A man is the last thing I'm looking for, but I'm not a fool, either. "Sure," I hear myself saying from a great distance as I levitate over the Valentine Party, something I have been doing a lot lately.

Soon after that I have to go to a meeting at N.C. State, so I meet Hal for lunch at a restaurant in Raleigh. But I am so nervous, I lean forward right in the middle of this lunch and say, "Well, how do you think this is going? Because I'm so nervous I would just as soon bag it if we're not having fun." Hal says he is having fun, so I keep on seeing him.

"Cut it out," my friends say. "This is supposed to be your interim man."

I write a song named "Interim Man." I keep on seeing Hal.

SUMMER 1981

Hal's daughter, Amity, is ten and very beautiful, all legs and big blue eyes, very feminine and very sophisticated. An only child, she has spent lots of time with adults, especially her adoring father. This is the first entire summer day she has spent alone with me, while my boys are at a tennis day camp and her father is in Raleigh at work.

"Well, Amity, what would you like for lunch?" I ask her. "Would you rather have a grilled cheese sandwich or a peanut butter and jelly sandwich?"

She hesitates. "How about brie and French bread?" she says, used to little gourmet picnics with her dad.

All I have is Velveeta and Wonder.

But we bridge the yawning culture gap between us as the summer goes on. For one thing, Amity actually likes to go to the grocery store with me, a thing my boys can't stand. And we both like to cook, especially cakes. We bake cake after cake for the ravenous boys while my visiting mother, a former home economics teacher, calls out measurements from her reclining position on the sofa.

All three of us—me, my mother, and Amity—read the *National Enquirer* and the *Midnight Sun* from cover to cover as soon as we get them home from the grocery store. We especially love UFO abductions and multiple births and anything at all about Elvis. (This *National Enquirer* habit is Amity's own mother's only complaint about my parenting skills . . . though Lord knows, she has plenty of other things to choose from as well.) But I claim that I am doing research for a novel named *Lives of the Stars* which turns out to be sort of true anyway.

One day, Hal and I are reading the newspaper and I read some genius person's column and say, "Guess what? There is no other word in the English language that rhymes with 'orange.'"

Hal thinks for a minute. "What about Warren G. Harding?" he says.

Okay. I am in love.

SPRING 1982

Hal and I are walking in the woods, following one of the green-space trails that run all over town, when suddenly we come upon a life-size concrete hippo, climbing out of Bolin Creek as if emerging from the Blue Nile. Oh no, I think stupidly, a hippo! Anything can happen in Chapel Hill. I realize that we'll probably get married.

JANUARY 1983

A Snapshot of the End of My Youth. Chapel Hill Community Center. A recreation-department basketball game is in progress. My son's team, the Tigers, is ahead by two points, but it's nip and tuck all the way. "Shoot, Monty, shoot!" yells somebody's father, sitting next to me. For some reason, I turn around and look at this father. He's an attractive black man wearing a leather hat and a diamond ring. For some reason, he looks familiar. Then it hits me. It's Doug Clark! Of Doug Clark and the Hot Nuts! He's got a kid, Monty, on the opposing team. . . . *Oh no*, I am really old.

SUMMER 1983. THE BEEHIVE.

I drive from my house on Burlage Circle over toward the university on Franklin Street along those old stone walls on a hot green summer day which reminds me of that first time I ever came to Chapel Hill for summer school so long ago. Now I am going to visit Dr. Louis Rubin who has retired from teaching English (and southern literature, which he invented) in order to start a publishing company, of all things. It is located in a woodshed behind his old stone house on Gimghoul Road. A sign on the fence reads: "Algonquin Books of Chapel Hill, Editorial Offices. Please Keep Gate Closed Against Dog."

Louis Rubin was my creative writing teacher at Hollins for four years, which is why I still call him Mr. Rubin—I couldn't call him Louis if my life depended upon it. Mr. Rubin was a great, great teacher who changed my life, as he has changed so many others. In fact it is probable that I would never have become a writer at all if I had not encountered him when I did, because I was a wild girl, and I'm not sure what would have happened to me. But I do know for sure that if I am ever able to write anything real, or beautiful, or honest—anything that ever speaks truly about the human condition—it will be due to this man.

I enter carefully through the gate and go into the woodshed.

It's like a beehive in here. I say hello to Mimi Fountain, also from Hollins, Ann Moss, and Garrett Epps. Shannon Ravenel, Mr. Rubin's partner in this enterprise, works from St. Louis. Mr. Rubin has just written her a letter about their new venture: "This is going to be fun, I think." In the newspaper he has said, "Editing is just like teaching, but publishing is something else. I don't want to just put new people into print; I want to launch them." Right now, Mr. Rubin is making a peanut butter sandwich on top of an old filing cabinet in the back where he eats it, standing up. He does this every day. All around him, manuscripts rise to his knees.

The FedEx man comes in and the dog runs out, then we all

run out after the dog. The postman comes. Eva Rubin drives back from her job teaching political science at N.C. State. She waves and goes in the house, followed by the miscreant dog. Now Mr. Rubin feeds the birds, which means throwing several handfuls of seed straight up into the air. The sky goes black with birds and beating wings. I start squealing and batting at them. Mr. Rubin is laughing. Finally the birds fly away and he looks at me. "Whatcha got?" he asks and I hand him the pages I've brought, all wrinkled up and sweaty from me holding them.

I follow him inside the house to his office, where he sticks a cigar in his mouth and sits down and starts reading immediately. Mr. Rubin never does anything later. "I know it's got too many voices in it," I say when he gets done, but he grins and hands it back.

"Keep on going," he says, which is all he needs to say and all I need to hear, because I am already thinking what comes next, and I can't even remember driving home.

JUNE 29, 1985

Amity, age thirteen and very grown up, has specified a church wedding for her father and me, and so here we are at the Chapel of the Cross, rehearsing hurriedly for our tiny 10:00 A.M. ceremony, which will take place in less than an hour. Radiant in her white dress, Amity walks endlessly up and down the aisle carrying her bouquet, carrying herself just so. She looks beautiful. But the ladies arranging the flowers at the altar scowl at her, whispering among themselves, casting dark looks at the middle-aged groom.

Finally one of the ladies says acidly to me, "Just how old is she, anyway?" and I realize that they think she's the bride, not me in my green linen dress. Oh no. This is what I get for fancying myself a bride at my age! I ought to know better. I ought to stay single and write novels out in the woods.

But then, forty minutes later, I am the bride, and I am the

happiest bride ever, as the organ plays and the bells ring and we step out into the bright June day married, of all things, and my boys wave at some other boys who are skating on skateboards down Franklin Street.

THANKSGIVING 1985, 1986, 1987, 1988 . . .

For years we hold the Wild Turkey Classic every Thanksgiving. Originally it was Hal's idea to go out and play a couple innings of softball before the big traditional dinner in the afternoon. I jumped right on it. Genius! A morning softball game gives the kids and the visiting relatives and friends something to do (and keeps us all from drinking too much) during those long hours while the turkey roasts and those floats roll interminably down Fifth Avenue on TV. The baseball diamond at Phillips Junior High is right up the street. Hal makes some calls, especially to other diehard Durham Bulls fans like himself. I tell friends and neighbors. I make the dressing and mash the potatoes ahead of time.

Thanksgiving Day dawns clear and cold with a brilliant Carolina blue sky. Hal heads for the field early, taking bats and bases and gloves and his brother Jeff, who is reputed to have been scouted by the Yankees, but right now he's hung over. Hal pushes him out the door, not easy. I've already got the turkey in the oven, covered with tons of butter and several old kitchen towels and tin foil—my substitute for basting. I corral the wild boys and fill up the station wagon with dogs, kids, juice, store-bought donuts and coffeecake, and a folding table to put it all out on. We turn right off Estes and head up to the raised grassy baseball field, which looms like some kind of Indian mound or ancient fort. Coming up over the hill, I stop amazed at the scene before me, like a Brueghel painting. Who are all these people? I guess the word spread. People are everywhere, doing knee bends, running, tossing the ball back and forth, talking, hugging, hugging. Lots of hugging. I set up my table and talk intensely with friends I haven't seen for years. People spread quilts on the sidelines. Somebody has brought a brand new baby in a little yellow suit; he is passed around and admired. Laughter rings out like bells. Our breath makes white puffs in the chilly blue air, cartoon conversation. Kids and dogs cover the outfield. Now whistles are blowing. They're already choosing sides. It's Michael McFee vs. Jay Bryant—two poets! Whoever thought the poets would be competitive? But they're cool, choosing wimpy kids like my own as well as grown-ups. Each side has got about thirty players. Bill Leuchtenburg, in his seventies, is playing second. Jimmy Mills, very slightly younger, is at third. A huge scream goes up when a yellow lab snatches the ball and runs off into the trees with it.

"PLAY BALL!" somebody hollers, and then we do, for the next twenty years or so, as the Massengale boys and the Ludingtons grow up before our very eyes and other kids go away and get married and then come back with their own kids, first in strollers and then on the field, another generation. Some people divorce and return with other people. Some people go to graduate school in Iowa, or to rehab, or New York or Asheville or Austin, places too far to come back from. Every year, more girls are playing, not only our perennial Elva, a ringer. Bill Leuchtenburg is still playing second. Jim Watson still bikes to the game wearing that Duke hat, his hair flying out behind him. All of Amity's boyfriends have to come and play ball, this is a requirement. On and on it goes, year after year, on sunny Thursdays and cloudy Thursdays and freezing Thursdays, in fog, in sleet, the sweet taste of donuts, the crack of the bat, the screams and yells and laughter of the crowd, old friends and new, all these dear and changing faces, these lovers of the game.

JUNE 2012

Hal and I have lived in Hillsborough for sixteen years now, so it's not often I find myself driving alone through Chapel Hill this late at night, windows down, after a concert with friends. I glimpse a little sliver of moon above the moving treetops. Maybe because it's that precious time at the end of the semester before summer school has started, but it's quiet as quiet can be tonight on Franklin Street, no people and no other cars, only a little breeze rustling the thick leaves on all these big trees and bringing me the unbearably sweet and somehow sad scent of honeysuckle. This reminds me of eating dinner one June night at Crook's Corner when Bill Smith had just invented his famous honeysuckle sorbet, which he brought out to our table. And it was true, I could taste it, all the inexpressible longing of honeysuckle as it melted on my tongue. Now the breeze brings laughter and music from far away. All those years, all that music, starting with Bland Simpson and Jim Wann's early '70s performance of *Diamond Studs* at the Old Ranch House restaurant on Airport Road, everybody dancing on the tables to "Cakewalk in Kansas City." I had never seen anything like it, "musicians' theater" they called it, and they would take it straight to Broadway. Then later, *King Mackerel and the Blues Are Running*, with Don Dixon . . . and always, Jim Watson's annual Christmas show at the Cave . . . and Callie Warner singing the title song "Good Ol Girls" for our own show in its first production at Swain Hall right on the UNC campus. I remember Tommy Thompson singing his "Hot Buttered Rum," one of the most beautiful songs in the world, at the old Cat's Cradle in the dead of winter. Most of all I remember my son Josh sitting down at the piano in Akai Hana sushi restaurant to play his own signature jazz set, "Five Not So Easy Pieces" he used to call it, which always included "Pachelbel," those running purely joyous notes, a celebration. The music of this night comes closer now, and the laughter, and then I see them, barefooted girls four abreast walking down the middle of the street, long hair swinging, singing. That blonde, second from the left, looks somehow familiar to me as she doubles over in laughter and almost falls. Oh she's got no idea what's going to happen to her in the years to come, and she doesn't care, either. All she wants is now, and she wants it bad, and I want her to have it all. But then the van ahead of me stops to let some people out, and when I can see again, they're gone, those girls, *she's* gone, my girl, if she ever was there at all.

My Mind Grinds the Graveyard

CLYDE EDGERTON

In a cotton patch, belonging to my grandfather (born 1865), a field hand pitched over, dying. Then he lay dead between rows. Nobody knew where Stanley was from or where to find his family. So he was buried behind the house in a field. Soon a cousin was born dead and buried beside him. A family graveyard was thus under way. Carved in the stone beside the baby's grave is this: "Born Ded."

When I was a child visiting the graveyard, the "Born Ded" could be traced with fingers, read clearly. Now, it is barely visible.

This graveyard, from my mother's side, sits about two miles south of the visitor's center in William B. Umstead State Park, between Durham and Raleigh, North Carolina, off highway 70. Twenty-six graves, resting in a square about the size of a big house foundation, sit off a trail that is graveled and wide enough for auto traffic, a trail used by hikers and bikers these days. Most of the park is gated—no cars or trucks.

Ah, a memory about that trail—but first a fact: during the Civil War it was a part of the Hillsborough-Raleigh Road. In my youth—the nineteen fifties and sixties—when the park was wide open and you could drive through it, that road was a normal gravel road. Another fact (I am getting to that memory in just a minute): it was the road that Sherman and his troops used late in the war when they were headed to Durham to accept Confederate General Johnston's surrender, and that brings me to a second memory before I get to the first. That second memory is the memory of hearing a certain family story at least twenty times, maybe fifty, from family members who are dead and gone. (I'm so sorry, but that brings to mind the memory of a story Eudora Welty once told of a man born during the Civil War. His last name was Floyd, and his full name was Elder Brother Come To Tell You All Your Friends Are Dead And Gone Floyd. They called him El.) So now that second memory:

But since I'm onto my great-grandmother, and prior to going back to that first memory, I have to tell you my great-grandmother's name and just a tiny bit about her. Please remember that what I'm writing about is a graveyard and the road beside it — a graveyard under tall pines, pines that are no longer ragged and dying because of the great vines of wisteria that ran all through them like anger, vines with vine descendants that covered acres, wisteria that started, as my mother used to say, pointing from the graveyard, rake handle in her other hand, " . . . right over there, where grandma planted a little wisteria vine, and I remember the trellis it grew on." After all the houses were torn down (1938–39), that vine and its descendants spread through the woods and up into trees around the graveyard and vacant homesites until sometime in the 1990s when workers cut them back in order to save choked trees.

So her name, my great-grandmother's, was Elizabeth Darbee Barbara Ferebee Caroline Jane Keith Warren. How many times have I said this follow-up true fact (I'll be telling you facts, as well as true facts, as well as memories): her husband, my great-granddaddy William Pinkney Warren, a millwright (b. 1826, when Tommy Jefferson and Sally Hemings were alive), called her "Puss." Their grandson, my great-uncle Alfred, his wife, Nora, and their ten children lived in the home place when the field hand, Stanley, was buried out back, the original grave. He's the only non-family member in the graveyard. (You don't have to remember these names.)

In 1936, the federal government bought up the whole area (5,000 acres) of what is now Umstead Park, tore down all stores and farm buildings and churches, and sold the land to North Carolina for a dollar. The land was depleted, farmed out. Now it's just woods where you can find occasional rock remnants of home foundations and piles of rocks from the clearing of fields for plowing, and if an early or late sun is at the right angle, you can make out cotton rows beneath pine straw from trees that are almost eighty years old.

When I see the place in my mind—that graveyard, that road—the stories start coming, as you've no doubt noticed. That's because my people had a habit of telling stories about the place, about nearby creeks, Crabtree and Sycamore. About the Sorrell store, the Adams store. About people: Uncle Alfred, Aunt Scrap, Mellie, Aunt Sara, who had a black dog named Sailor in her one-room house and when she told him to get out the door, he'd get under the table and she'd say, "Well, get under the table then." Stories told about the schoolhouse, the Moravian church. (Called the "Marvin" church by a relative whose name I've forgotten. She had a way with words, I've been told. Called a miracle a "mackerel." "It was just a mackerel he even got out of bed." She was fuzzy on Columbus's name, but she was clear on his bravery. She'd say to someone who was reluctant about something, "Aw, come on, take a chance—Columbia did.")

I will immediately get back to that first memory, I promise, but first I must tell you about the baby fingers. Elizabeth (the great-grandmother with all the names) was a midwife. She once birthed a baby who had twelve fingers. She cut off the two extras and put them in a little jar of alcohol which she hid behind a clock on the mantle for many years, and the children, including my mother (b. 1904), stood on a chair, delicately retrieved the jar, sat on the floor and looked into it the way kids today sit on the couch and stare into an iPod.

I can't say "kids" without thinking of Uncle Alfred's. The great-uncle with the ten kids, married to Nora. He was my granddaddy's brother (again, don't worry about keeping up with the family names—we are talking memory and *place*). I've heard so many stories about Uncle Alfred that he was one of my favorite uncles even though he died before I was born.

Pictures of the home place and the graveyard and stories of people and places as they existed in the community (Cedar Fork Township) of the graveyard can be found in a fantastic book called *Stories in Stone*, written by historian Tom Webber and published by the Umstead Coalition (umsteadcoalition. org), a group that watches over the park nowadays. If you want to see Umstead Park from above, go to Raleigh on your Google Map. Look to the northeast, toward Durham. See that giant green area between Durham and Raleigh? That's Umstead Park—it's what the Umstead Coalition (and our state government) is protecting, and if you think attacks have not been (and are being) plotted by hungry entrepreneurs, then keep watching. I just this minute saw the park on Google Map for the first time. I thought about the aunts and uncles—long gone—who cleaned the graves, and somehow the sight of the place from above, preserved to a degree, almost brought tears of sadness. Then I thought about my children, grandchildren to come, maybe—and I felt better, knowing they would have this place, these stories, preserved, like those baby fingers.

At the annual family graveyard cleaning in May, I can always find a youngin who's not heard some of the stories. Remembering the ones who told them to me, looking at the tall pines and the red clay and tombstones, and the food over on blankets, smelling the woods, and listening to the breeze through the pine needles—all this makes me know why people sometimes fight tooth and nail, finger and bone, for a place—a river, an island, a wall.

But about those ten kids of Alfred's. There in the kitchen of the old house with the graveyard out back, the kids, Alfred, and Aunt Nora ate meals around a long wooden table with benches. And Uncle Alfred, before coming in from the fields, would holler to Nora, "Muh, put on the coffee." She would, and as Uncle Bob (b. 1896), a main family storyteller, would say to me, "And Clyde, he'd come in in a little while and get that coffee pot from over the fireplace and it'd be going ba-lup, ba-lup, ba-lup, perking you know, and he'd put it to his lips and . . . and sip. Yessir. And that's a true fact."

The road by the graveyard, the one that spurred that first memory up at the top of this essay that I'm getting very close to—that road has a hill rising to the graveyard from the south, and Uncle Bob, about a hundred years ago, when he came home in the Model-T Ford, the gas tank almost on empty, couldn't drive forward up the hill lest the gravity-fed fuel system would fail. So he'd drive up the hill backwards. Or that's the story.

We are back in the road, and that brings me back to that first memory way up top:

Aunt Oma (b. 1899) stood in that road one day—this was probably about 1988. She said, "Come here."

I walked to her.

She said, "See in the woods there?" She pointed into the woods across from the graveyard. "See that ditch in there running along parallel to the road like it belongs to another road?"

"Yes ma'am."

"Well, can you kind of see what was a road in there—see how it kind of has a bank and a ditch along in some places?"

"Yes, ma'am, I can."

"That's where the old plank road was. From back before the Civil War. They used to talk about it."

The old plank road. Before the Civil War.

And right now, because it's in a state park, no strip-mall parking lot with a Toys "R" Us and a bank lies over the old plank-road site. What you saw on your Google Map, if you looked, what lies outside the green, will *remain* outside the green if those of us who believe in green conservative themes keep our voice and have our way. Our government saved my place, my family graveyard. Family stories would have survived without that graveyard, without the old homesite, but there would be no *place to hold the stories*. And so many of the stories—reshaped, the memories redefined, the memories of memories (sometimes reshaped a little, sometimes a lot)—thread through my novels and short stories—like a wisteria vine through pines.

One more memory about that road, the trail, now existing by the graveyard: about 100 yards to the northwest, in the woods just beside the trail, is an indention. If you look carefully, you will see big rocks around the edges. The indention was once an open well, lined with rocks. That well was the burial spot of Piddle Diddle, Uncle Bob's pet rooster. One day Piddle Diddle chased a hen that flew over the well opening. Piddle Diddle followed, but didn't quite make it. He fell into the well and drowned. End of story. We must adopt an abrupt stop, else this may go on forever.

To have a place is to have yourself in spite of the uncertainty and void of the universe. Thus, to have a place is to have the start of story.

The School of Generosity

LYDIA MILLET AND JENNY OFFILL

Lydia Millet and Jenny Offill, novelists and close friends, sat down recently to talk about their time at UNC–Chapel Hill, where they both studied fiction as undergraduates in the late 1980s.

LYDIA: So we were both at Chapel Hill from 1986 to 1990, and we were both already writing fiction, but our lives only barely intersected then. I studied with Daphne Athas and you studied with Doris Betts; I ran in pretentious circles, where people played croquet and served mint juleps at Kentucky Derby parties, whereas you ran in hipper ones, involving bands called Teasing the Korean. I had a friend, back then, from high school that actually ended the friendship because I was too pretentious. That didn't slow me down, though; I kept on speaking in polysyllabic words and suspecting I might be a tragic poet. (You too, right?) I also sang opera at the time, mostly Verdi. You dated guys in bands, waited tables, and ran the literary magazine.

Our pretentious/down-to-earth polarity would shortly reverse itself, though: by the time we met again, through our former teacher Jill McCorkle, in California in the early 1990s—when we became close, as we have been ever since—my life was anything but pretentious, whereas yours was a bit gilded. I was working a drudge job as a copyeditor at *Hustler* magazine, a bottom feeder in Larry Flynt's smut-magazine workforce in Los Angeles, whereas you were at Stanford consorting with other members of the Stegner set. You were the chosen people by then; I was the worker bee.

But at UNC, just a couple of years before finding myself accepting a job at *Hustler,* I was dreaming of lofty heights. Some of my friends were even European.

JENNY: You were very intimidating, I thought. I remember you submitted a poem to *Cellar Door* that was about a middle-aged couple returning from a party and climbing the stairs to bed with great resignation. You sounded like you were already 100 years old, and I both admired and made fun of how sophisticated you seemed. I had not yet started muttering darkly about my own unrecognized genius, but the seeds of it were being planted.

I had gone to UNC planning to be an actress, but then freshman year I took an intro to creative writing class with James Seay and was very taken with it and with him. That eye patch and that droll voice! It fixed in my head forever what sort of dashing figure a writer should be. Little did I know that years later I would spend all my time in torn sweatpants and my husband's sweaters, writing in a curtained-off part of the laundry room.

But UNC was such a great place for experimenting and testing out new ideas. I was lucky enough to have Doris Betts as my next teacher (she had also taught my father many years before), and I remember how excited I would be if she wrote a "good" in the margin of one of my stories. Mostly she wrote "aargh" though. I do recall that one of my first stories featured a timid schoolgirl turned Vegas dancer who dyed her hair "the color of summer squash." Clearly I was not a believer in the "write what you know" school.

LYDIA: And I was still worse, because before the sonnet about middle-aged marital weariness I wrote stories of postapocalyptic mother-daughter teams who ran around spearing giant cockroaches and eking out a living among gently radioactive ash-can fires. Daphne Athas, as I recall, had some kind words about that one—words to the general effect of, "Despite the content, style, and lexicon of this, I see a glint here of a mind at work."

Her honesty, paired with the hope she held out eternally that gold would be spun from straw, was probably the thing that made me keep writing back then. She has the great gift of being able to see promise in something that, to the layperson's eye, would look strikingly similar to a dung heap.

For me, Chapel Hill was a deeply romantic place, as soon as I got away from the dorms and could walk its pleasant streets in what felt more like adult company. Or alone. It's crucial to be alone sometimes, at that age. And later. I hope it's still romantic to those who arrive there now—I hope they can see past the chain stores crowding Franklin Street to the beauty of those old trees, for instance, the maples, the soaring oaks and beeches and hollies on those idyllic grounds that used to create, at least in my mind, a kind of shady green bower scenario. I hope all that prenostalgic ideation isn't gone. Because the main job of liberal-arts colleges, it seems to me—and one UNC did so well—is to allow a heroic narrative of the self to be written, so that in subsequent years there are the remains of a proud monument against which the sands of life can wash up.

JENNY: A heroic narrative of the self, indeed! I find that even now, a certain slant of light through leaves reminds me of how I used to walk across that lovely campus, feeling as if my brain were on fire from all the things I was reading and thinking. Particular lines of poetry that I learned in those years have stayed with me. All have a certain sweeping drama that befits the heroic narrative I was building. For example, Dylan Thomas's "Time held me green and dying / Though I sing in my chains like the sea."

Or from Yeats's "Sailing to Byzantium": "Consume my heart, sick with desire / and fastened to a dying animal"

Or Auden's "We too make noises when we laugh or weep / Words are for those with promises to keep."

All of this thrilled, and I can remember coming out of Greenlaw Hall after one English class or another and feeling electrified by the realization that anything, anything at all, could be of interest if a writer transformed it with the force of his attention. Later you told me that one of your professors had told you that he had been through terrible hardships, but once he found "the life of the mind," he was saved. That it would always be a source of great solace.

We may have laughed a little at the earnest phrase, but the truth is we both believed in such a thing. I've always felt saved by books, though God knows, back then I had no particular hardships I needed to triumph over.

LYDIA: Dying and death, death and dying. Those years were the long, pure moment when our mortality dawned, right? These days it's overhead and maybe casts a bleaker, plainer light, but when it first truly dawned, after childhood, the sky was pretty glamorous. There was a breeze that sprang up and stripes of purple and red.

I loved the writing classes I took at UNC, too—with Elizabeth Spencer, Jill McCorkle, Robert Kirkpatrick, and of course Daphne, who was my mentor and has encouraged me my whole life. Even this year, she sent me encouraging, invigorating e-mails. Oddly, after UNC I never liked another workshop. There was an openness and permeability to the teaching and learning culture I never met with again.

And I don't think it was just the romanticism of being eighteen, nineteen, twenty—I think it was those professors, who were so dear and so devoted to their students.

JENNY: I felt very lucky to have the professors I had in the UNC writing program: James Seay, Doris Betts, Robert Kirkpatrick, Jill McCorkle, Marianne Gingher. They all had very different styles, but each of them had a combination of generosity and rigor that I think is what makes a workshop come alive and be more than an echo chamber of praise or criticism. I've taught now for many years, and I think I still use a lot of what I learned there.

Kirkpatrick had that unerring eye for nonsense, and he would write little witty comments in the margin when one's flights of poetic fancy had landed with a particularly loud thud. I can still remember how my cheeks would burn when I read his thoughtful but somehow devastating comments. But he could also be incredibly encouraging. He told me that I should be a writer very early on, and though this seemed a crazy idea, it was also thrilling. And Doris Betts was kind enough to tell my parents that she had faith in me, too. I try now for that same mix of carrot and stick with my students. I'm hardest on the talented ones, but I try to take them all seriously. That was a real gift I got from the UNC writing faculty—the gift of being taken seriously long before I'd really proved I should be.

That's the generosity I'm speaking of, but I think if it had come in the form of praise only, I would have discounted it. To write something that's surprising and true and mysterious and strange is so difficult. I felt encouraged to experiment there, to risk falling on my face. So many writing workshops these days feel professionalized, all about "the marketplace" and what will sell: blah, blah, blah. None of that ever crept in there, and I do my best to keep it out of my workshops, too. The other day I told my Columbia students I would give them the secret of how to make it as a writer. There were two, I claimed. (They all leaned forward, ready to write them down.) Number 1 was, learn how to live very cheaply and not worry about it. Steal cheese from parties! Eat in the Hare Krishna tent! The second was, allow everyone you know to believe you are a complete failure for at least ten years and revel in their pity as a sign you are doing it right, that you are taking the long apprenticeship of becoming a writer seriously.

They looked at me quizzically. No one wrote anything down.

LYDIA: Your rules are so beautifully simple the students didn't need to write them down. It's like, for instance, $E=mc^2$. Who needs to write that down? And I like the fact that you drew from your own experience in issuing those edicts. Clearly you've come a long way since the days when you wrote about hair the color of summer squash.

I have to be honest here: I only went to UNC because I was rejected by every other school I applied to. Sometimes when I say that, people think I'm exaggerating, but really, no, because no other university accepted me, not a single one in these United States, nor any other country. And I used to suspect the only reason Chapel Hill agreed to have me was that my maternal grandfather, a good-natured Georgia peach farmer, had also gone there in his youth. Briefly. This would have been maybe 1929, 1930. Apparently he was kicked out for punching a professor, or at least that's how the family lore goes. The story goes that this professor, who shall remain nameless mostly because no one has ever told me his name, accused Papa of cheating after he performed above expectations on a chemistry test. And because Papa was a country gentleman, he was forced to defend his honor/answer with violence. But it didn't go over well, finally, the fist-to-face approach, and so he left the ivory tower, never to return.

I've been convinced ever since my college days that this rejection by other schools and acceptance by Chapel Hill was a great stroke of luck for me—not only because it made me correctly humble but also because it put me in a place where I would be inspired and happy and surrounded by these extraordinarily gracious teachers. I mean, of course I had some bad times—heartbreak is on the core curriculum in college, isn't it, along with other unpleasant subjects? I had a handsome boyfriend, an actor with long hair from an exotic country who dumped me my junior year for a rich girl who'd gone to an elite eastern prep school, referred glancingly to her tragic cocaine past, and had already done all twelve steps by the time I drank my first jug of Ernest & Julio.

At the time, this was discouraging, yes. But when I look back, I feel a clear appreciation for it, a kind of admiration, frankly. Because even as this mandatory course in abandonment was occurring, I was learning the life of the mind, as Sid Smith and you put it—I was learning that although we remain alone in our bodies, our minds and their great hopes and grief gather together in the spaces of books. And there, the lonely are legion.

26 Miles

JUDY GOLDMAN

Driving to Charlotte was a big deal.

Such a big deal that Mother put on a hat.

Such a big deal, the trip had its own set of rituals.

As we drove over the Catawba River Bridge, on the outskirts of Rock Hill, a mile before the Carolinas border, Mother, my sister Brenda, or I would comment: "River's high today." To be followed by one of us confirming: "Really high." Or, if rocks were visible in the water (muddy-red from the South Carolina clay), one of us would say, "Gosh, the river sure is low today." When we returned home at dusk, we'd remark again on the river's rise or fall.

Another ritual was just between Brenda and me: Fort Mill was the only town we passed on our way to Charlotte. Brenda and I would tsk-tsk over how sorry we felt for the people who had to live there (a touch of disdain mixed in). "So tiny, so podunk," Brenda would say with a sniff. "Thank goodness we live in Rock Hill," I'd say, thrilled to conspire about *any*thing (even a town) with my sister, who was three years older and a real expert. I then, of course, would produce my own sniff.

Maybe people in South Carolina were unusually competitive in the forties. Or maybe we were just trying to get a leg up. After all, South Carolina's school system was so bad (second to bottom on every list), we had to redeem ourselves with, *Thank goodness for Mississippi.* Truth is, Fort Mill was a town not much smaller—and no more podunk—than Rock Hill. (Years later, Fort Mill would leapfrog to worldwide fame over Rock Hill, thanks to Jim and Tammy Faye Bakker's PTL Club at Heritage USA.)

Once inside Charlotte's city limits, our route took us past a gray-and-white contemporary house, which we knew was Mother's dream house. She'd slow down to a turtle's pace, her foot tapping the brake, the gas, the brake, so that she could take in details she might have missed last time—the modern circular driveway which no one in Rock Hill even thought of having, the gray stonework, the front yard, all grass, no trees to speak of, just bushes, no flowers.

We lived in an older, two-story, white clapboard house with grey shutters. In spring, tulips, cupped and elaborate, circled the huge oak in the front yard. Forsythias bloomed by the driveway, yellow as stars. Brenda and I paid the most attention to the dogwood trees. I'm not sure how many years in a row we poured bottles of Mercurochrome into the roots, determined to turn the white blossoms pink. We loved that house, which I'd lived in since birth: the knotty pine den with its floor-to-ceiling bookshelves, family photographs in bamboo frames covering the wall around the mantel, the row of African violets lining the double windowsills, Brenda's and my desks facing opposite corners. We even loved the living room, which we entered only to practice our duets or to hear Mother playing the one song she knew. No one actually sat on the hand-carved mahogany sofa, but Brenda and I could make each other laugh so hard we practically stopped breathing just by repeating what Mother always said when we made fun of that stiff, uncomfortable piece of furniture: "You know who made this? Mr. *Weinsel!*" She enunciated his name so meticulously, so vigorously, she could've been telling us President Truman made the sofa. But the space closest to Brenda's and my hearts was the bedroom we shared, our bachelor-button wallpaper, twin beds and matching wedding-ring quilts, the fireplace, our square little closets with their faceted glass doorknobs.

It made no sense whatsoever for Mother to covet a brand new, cold, modern, one-story house when she already owned a warm, cozy, older house on a street with long wooded views.

Why would she want to break the mold of the familiar? Heck, our address was even Eden Terrace.

After a morning of shopping at Ivey's Department Store on Tryon Street, we would eat lunch—rare roast beef sliced while we stood there, waiting—at the S&W Cafeteria. Or maybe we'd have something dainty at the Tulip Terrace upstairs in Ivey's, where a woman played the piano. (One of my long-range ambitions still is to play the piano in a restaurant, like her.) Our favorite lunch place, though, was around the corner from Ivey's: The Oriental. It was dimly lit (was it smoky?), the atmosphere a little shady, a bit doubtful. Each table was hidden away, enclosed in tufted red partitions. Johnny Tom, the owner, moved through the place with smooth, calculated, purposeful movements, his shoes clicking over the white, octagonal-tiled floor. There were rumors the restaurant was actually a secret Chinese gambling hall.

Brenda and I shared an order of chow mein. Mother got her own. And, of course, we each had a Coke. My mother believed in Coca Cola. Once, after taking care of my father's sister when she was dying of cancer, Mother wrote a letter to the president of Coca-Cola, thanking him for his "life-saving drink." She told him that sips of Coke had kept her sister-in-law alive longer than anyone expected.

After lunch we'd walk back to Ivey's—maybe to reconsider a dress or skirt we'd been unsure about before, when we were too hungry to think. Then, out the heavy front doors, a left turn down Tryon Street, half a block to Al Goodman Shoes. Al Goodman was a small man with a gravelly voice and a New York accent. Brenda and I would sometimes *be* him when we played store in our backyard playhouse: "Peggy! Thisss isss a hot look," we'd say, hissing the way he did. (Back then, people's teeth didn't always fit right.) "A very hot look for ssspring!" Mother said he had a heart of gold. But then, Mother thought everyone had a heart of gold.

A few doors down from Al Goodman Shoes was . . . Montaldo's. The ellipses were always present in any sentence that included the word, *Montaldo's*. Once, Mother stepped out of Ivey's onto the sidewalk, and a guy grabbed her pocketbook. She was so shocked (*flabbergasted!* her word, her exclamation point), she immediately reached right out and grabbed it back. She then ran down Tryon, clutching the pocketbook to her breast, never looking back, all the way to . . . Montaldo's. I'm sure her thinking was, there, in that rarefied atmosphere, she'd be safe. Montaldo's . . . opened in 1919 by two sisters, Lillian and Nelle Montaldo. (Maybe the fact that two sisters owned the store added to its appeal for us.) Mother, Brenda, and I always took a few minutes to admire the ceiling—the painted, pale blue sky and ample, white mountains of clouds. You'd have thought the whole world was rotating right inside that Italian Renaissance Revival building. The salesladies knew Mother by name, and she knew theirs, as well as their children's names, and any illnesses they might have had. Ever. The air smelled perfumed, powdery, like someone's dressing table. The shoe department was hushed, peaceful. Upstairs: racks of dresses, blouses and skirts, suits and coats, evening gowns. I can still see the Montaldo's label, with its distinctive zigzag, rickrack stitching. Nothing bad could ever happen in . . . Montaldo's.

Here's the thing about Charlotte: it was the place you went to when you needed someone who really knew what they were doing. Brenda's orthodontist was in the Doctor's Building in Charlotte. Sure, my friends and I could see Arthur Smith and the Crackerjacks perform in the Rock Hill High School auditorium, but to see Elvis Presley we had to get someone's older sister to drive us to the Coliseum on Independence Boulevard in Charlotte. Elvis wasn't the only star my friends and I saw at the Coliseum. There were all those rock-and-roll shows. I still have my autograph from Shirley of Shirley and Lee ("Let the Good Times Roll"): *To Judy, be good always, Shirley.*

Now, move forward through the years. Brenda and I are in our thirties, each of us married. I have two young children, Brenda four. Our parents are going through the process of dying at the same time. Mother has Alzheimer's and doesn't recognize anyone. She can't *see* at all. She can't speak; all she can do is moan. Our father's colon cancer has metastasized to his lungs and bones. I could easily take to my bed, but instead, I take to my typewriter. I write poem after maudlin poem. I attend the Duke University Writers' Workshop, with Sir Stephen Spender as my instructor. He actually seems to like my poems. He calls them "lovely watercolors about a quaint little village."

But I no longer live in that "village." My husband, Henry, and I live in the big city of Charlotte, blocks away from Brenda and her husband. Mother is in a nursing home here. Our father alternates staying with Brenda and then me because he's too weak to drive back and forth between Rock Hill and Charlotte, and he wants to spend all day, every day, at Mother's bedside.

No matter what I write, the setting is always Rock Hill: in my poetry. Later, the novels. Still later, my memoir.

Which is why I want to say something here about landscape.

From the outside looking in, it doesn't appear as though I've changed my landscape to any great degree. I didn't pack my bags and move to Paraguay. All I did was travel a few miles over the state line. Of course, there were stops along the way, intervening years. I graduated from college in Georgia, taught high school English in Atlanta, worked in film and then advertising in New York City. But one evening, when a fortune-teller at the Copacabana in Manhattan read the creases of my palm and saw a tall, handsome, red-headed man in my future—and a tall, handsome, red-headed man miraculously appeared a week later in the form of a blind date while I was home visiting my parents between jobs—I ended up in Charlotte, with that man, twenty-six miles from Rock Hill, just over the Catawba River Bridge.

I'm not dizzyingly unmoored in a strange and foreign land. But the miles between my birthplace and my adopted (these forty-six years) homeland have given me the distance I need—not too much dislocation, but *enough*—to write about my loved ones and the familiar world left behind. Somehow, this New South City has enabled me to observe from the shadows of its tall buildings the mother who played "Humoresque" on the piano, whose chords brought the walls in around me like arms, who understood that a day she and my sister and I spent together = love. I can observe from the shadows a sister with whom I shared a room, an order of chow mein, and more. Observe a father, whom I describe in my memoir as being an Atticus Finch. A brother, older than Brenda and I, more sophisticated, and oh, how the two of us idolized him. I can describe—over and over—the house on Eden Terrace, the ground of intimacy on which my life story was built.

Writers don't need dramatic jumps in geography to help us tell how memory works. We can look back on the particulars of our lives simply by crossing a river.

Seven Postcards from an
Orange County Childhood

WELLS TOWER

1978

City water came to the sticks where we lived south of town. They dug a big hole at the end of my road. It filled up with pumpkin-colored water and for a couple of weeks we had a swimming pool. I would sneak out around dawn and go skinny-dip there in solitude before the neighborhood kids woke up. One morning, age five, I mooned a slowly passing Pontiac. On came the brake lights, beacon of panic to roadside misbehavers the world over. A drunken woman got out of the car and began to curse me. I do not think it was a dream that she was naked. She clutched to her nudeness a loose brown and yellow afghan the size a dish towel. I didn't know why she was so furious. Remorseful, I thought that somehow the sight of my nude bottom had magically deprived the woman of her clothes. Then a man got out of the driver's side. Giggling madly, he packed the naked lady back into the Pontiac and they went away.

1981

From my father's house, Knockwood's Sunoco lies about four miles, as the crow flies, or as the eight-year-old trots, his pockets swollen with one-hundred-and-three carefully counted, pilfered pennies making chain-mail cadence as he takes the long march. Fleeing marauding dogs across alien yards, weaseling over and under rusted barbed wire, through densities of ice-pick thistle, and consommé-colored trans-cowfield brooks, he holds the stressed pockets of his Lees. One-o-three is a magical figure, representing one Snicker bar, one Lance Choc-o-Mint, and a sixteen-ounce Cheerwine in the newfangled potbellied bottle, plus three cents tax. The boy is not so farsighted as to have stolen an extra coin or two from the father's hoard in the Danish cookie tin. Should a single cent leak from his jeans, the whole scheme is sunk. He stumbles along, clutching his pockets, an undercover noble-man fleeing the Jacobins.

Two hours later, he emerges from the forest, his Stride-Rites squirting cattle water, his arms graffitied up by thorns. He tracks wet footprints across Knockwood's store. Breathing hard, he sets his groceries on Mr. Knockwood's counter and stands up on tiptoes to disgorge all that heavy wealth. Knock-wood's deep-veed forehead is brick red and textured like a parched sponge. He looks down at the child's copper and he says, "I don't need all them pennies."

"What?"

"It'd about snap my drawer off if I put all them pennies in there. I don't need 'em."

The boy feels a fluttering panic that is nearly a kind of ec-stasy. "But, but, but . . ."

Folding money bears the language *legal tender for all debts*, and the boy understands that it is illegal for this Knockwood to refuse his good coin. His first impulse is to call the po-lice. His second is to weep. But before either of these things happens, the Budweiser delivery man says, "I'll take 'em." The driver puts down green money and rakes the hundred of brown money into a cupped hand. The boy experiences a kind of moral whiplash to have chanced across, in the same handful of seconds, so Satanic a fuckface as Knockwood, and then this trucker, a Jack Chick saint.

We actually lived next to some Knockwoods. They had been alone on the land next door to our property for several generations. They showed their resentment at our arrival indirectly by humiliating us in a series of undeclared competitions.

They beat us in firewood contests, felling trees along the property line, splitting the logs and stacking them to season in tidy, antler-colored pyramids that could have been on the cover of a magazine about rustic art. They beat us in contests of food abundance, filling the autumn air with the sound of shrieking hogs, a loud, panicked wail you'd not have thought possible from an animal with its throat cut. Every time I heard it I knew a terrible and brutal thing was happening at the Knockwood place, but I also knew that to be rich in slab bacon was a kind of wealth more pure and immediate than plain money, and I felt bested.

James Knockwood, the father, took special pleasure in beating us in knowledge competitions about the hardness of the world. He had a large, American build and lots of illegible tattoos, and he used to come around to tell us about assorted rough deeds he'd committed as the captain of a local motorcycle gang called the Broke Spoke Club. We also learned that during the war in Vietnam, he'd been forced to shoot a young woman who'd run at him with an explosive strapped to her chest. My mother said she'd rather get blown up than have something like that on her conscience. James Knockwood said, "I hate to tell you, Betsy, but you're naïve."

Most of my losses, though, were at the hands of the son, Jimmy Knockwood Jr. Two years older than me, Jimmy wore a hint of Iroquois aristocracy in his cheekbones, and some part of his body was usually sheathed in a dirty plaster cast. He beat me at every sport we had equipment for. At thirteen, he had arms like a man and could throw a baseball with such force that after playing catch with him, you couldn't hold a pencil. Once, when we were wrestling, he put me in a chokehold that made my vision go white. I cursed Jimmy's mother, and he rubbed a toad into my teeth. Seeing me in tears afterward, my father asked why I put myself through the disgrace of playing with Jimmy. He had forgotten the infatuation a boy has no choice but to feel for another boy who is good at everything.

Our last contest was on my twelfth Christmas. That morning I woke to a sound like a hornet swarm tearing through the Knockwood property. Twenty minutes later, before I'd opened my stocking, Jimmy came razzing over on a brand-new Kawasaki off-road motorbike. Sleek with chrome shocks and lustrous green fairings, it was a thing of lethal, insectile beauty—a cross between a dragonfly and a chainsaw.

"Race you," Jimmy said. "Come on, get your bike."

I said I couldn't see the sense in going up against that Kawasaki on my bicycle, a single-speed antique made of skillet metal and a child's model to boot.

"Aw, don't cry, turtle pecker," Jimmy said. "Pick your head start, long as you want. Plus I won't kick it out of first gear. Give you ten dollars, win or lose."

This was Jimmy's standard ploy: to lure you into unwinnable competitions by offering fraudulent, self-sacrificial conditions that could not be refused. I took the bait, and went to fetch my bike from the leaky shed where it had been rusting since summertime.

The neighbors' long and rutted driveway was the racecourse, the Knockwood mailbox the finish line. Jimmy's parents came out to watch the pointless spectacle, also his three sisters and a cheering horde of raw-boned cousins, uncles, and aunts. Winning was not a possibility, I knew; I was just desperate to get away from that hostile crowd. We lined up, and I gathered the nerve to ask for a ten-second lead. In lieu of a starter pistol, Jimmy's mother put her fingers in her mouth and let out a piercing whistle, and I ducked my head and went tearing down the driveway.

The group counted down my time while Jimmy revved and

grinned. At Mrs. Knockwood's second whistle blast, Jimmy kicked the Kawasaki into gear and wrung the throttle. The bike took off faster than he'd meant it to, shooting past me, past the edge of the driveway, jouncing over a tussocky side-yard, and rocketing deep into a house-high tangle of black-berry and honeysuckle vines, where the engine finally died. I kept cranking until I'd reached the mailbox, where I raised a tentative hand in victory.

No one was looking at me, though. James Knockwood had charged into the vinework tunnel the bike had bored to pull out his fallen son, who was moaning, his right hand hanging at a weird angle from his wrist. Then James Sr. retrieved the bike. The fork was bent, the front wheel folded into a taco shape. The paint job looked like someone had gone over it with a cat-o'-nine-tails. The gas cap was missing—the least of the Kawasaki's troubles, yet it was this detail that enraged Mr. Knockwood most. "Where's the gas cap at? Where's the goddamn gas cap, Jimmy?" Knockwood yelled, as though this were a question his son were capable of answering. With an open hand, he belted Jimmy a number of times in the face, using plenty of follow-through.

I went home feeling no joy whatsoever at having beaten Jimmy after a year of bruising losses. Rather, I felt queasy and wrong about having breached the good and natural order of life there on our hill, a presentiment, I guess, of Jimmy and his family's future. Things never quite turned around for the Knockwoods after Jimmy crashed the Kawasaki. The cancer must have already been well into Mr. Knockwood's brain that Christmas day, because by Easter he was a 110-pound skeleton and by summer he was dead. His widow scalped the land of its timber before selling the property to my parents.

1986

If you met somebody who was willing to "go" with you, what you did, you took her over to campus, to Coker Arboretum and got down in an ivy patch. Or friends of mine who had already done their share of living told me this was so. One night, I got somebody to go back there with me, and we necked for the first time in our lives. It was all pretty fine, but when I got out of there to see my friends, I couldn't brag to them about it. I thought my paws had mostly been on that girl, but from the look of them, they had mostly been in a fire-ant pile. A thousand insects had bitten my hands. They had swelled up very pink and very hot. "Little Smokies" is what my friends called my fingers. This was a kind of fluorescent sausage available at the Food Lion but not the Harris Teeter.

1987

Sometimes, out where we lived, you got so bored you had to call the cops on yourself, or get someone to do it for you.

Behind our house, there was our messy field and then a road, and then one of those new houses. The yard was the size of a pool table, and yet the owner scalped it daily on a lawn tractor. This seemed silly and disgusting to me and my brother who had to mow many rough acres with an ancient Briggs-and-Stratton Grunt-Behind. So one summer afternoon, we found some bottle rockets and sent two gross of them into our field, in hopes of knocking that householder off of his John Deere. It had been a dry summer, and before long, we were looking at a wall of fire twenty feet high. So my brother and I went into the house. I filled up a salad bowl with water. My brother topped up a couple of iced tea pitchers. My father did not smell the smoke and the sirens weren't in earshot yet. "What are you going to do with all that water?" he asked me.

"Oh, nothing in particular," I said.

1989

Before it was condominiums, you had "the Valley," a confidential kudzu jungle, accessible via an alley off of Rosemary

Street, right uptown. The Valley was a good prom night destination. You and your best ninth grade pal have somehow persuaded two eleventh grade punker girls to be your dates, or at least to be seen in the gym with you for five minutes, before you all sneak out the back. So then you go to the Valley, where you and your pal have stashed a case of hot Black Label beer down in the vines. Neither of you will be getting anywhere with those old and dangerous girls. In fact, they meet their Army boyfriends in the Valley, and the boyfriends drink most of your beer. Not all of it, though. Your friend gets good and drunk. At midnight, your friend's good mother, Leslie Ann, pulls up in front of the post office to ferry you and your dates back home.

You sit up front. Your pal sits in the back between the two famous beauties of the high school counterculture. Leslie Ann, who is almost your mother, too, has been out swing dancing, and she wants to talk about it. In the rearview, you notice that your friend has silently begun to vomit down the front of his rented tux.

"So tell me, Leslie Ann," you say to his mother, solicitous as any talk show host, "what exactly *is* swing?"

2013

Knockwood's Sunoco isn't there anymore. For a while it was Knockwood's Texaco, and then somebody else's BP, and now it's one of those places where they tore out the gas pumps, and they sell wines of the Loire Valley and local goat cheese and heirloom tomatoes for six dollars a pound.

This morning, I bump into Jimmy Knockwood Jr. in the Harris Teeter parking lot. He is still an acquaintance of mine. He's doing well for himself. He is a successful contractor and a maker of beautiful furniture I will never be able to afford. Today, he's got a new daughter in his truck. Three months old, with a feathery pelt of mouse-colored hair. Her lips are a shapely bow. Her eyelids nictitate to reveal a spooky white blankness, but she is smiling in her sleep.

He says, "This is little Flora. Maybe I told you, it was rough getting her into the world, but I don't think I told you how rough. I almost came back from the hospital alone. We were about eight months along, and one morning Sally, my wife, makes a noise in the shower. It's more than a whimper and less than a scream. I go in there. She says, 'We're going to the hospital. Get in the car. Now is not a time to drive the speed limit.'

"We get her to the hospital. They've just put her on the gurney when she just goes white as a piece of paper. Her heart rate's through the roof. The baby's is beating at 160. One-twenty's normal. They get her into the OR and do an emergency C-section. They get the baby out. No vital signs. And Sally's bleeding like you wouldn't believe. A gusher. The blood's just pouring out of her. They can't find where she's bleeding from. They just open her up and take everything out, but they still can't find it.

"Meanwhile, they resuscitate the baby, get her breathing, intubate her. The chaplain comes and finds me in the waiting room. I'm thinking, Sally, Flora, both of them, they're dead. They're gone. He asks if he can 'petition' for Sally and the baby. I'm like, 'I'm not really into that, but if you want to, sure, go ahead.'

"In the meantime, Sally's still bleeding. She goes through all the blood of her type they've got on hand. They have to bring in a filtration system, so they can just keep running her blood through it. She goes through the blood of nine adults. Eighty-three units. Finally, they find the bleeding. It's an aneurysm in her splenic artery, which runs between the aorta and the spleen. It's the size of a small water hose. They take her spleen out, get her stabilized. But when you're bleeding like that, it has all these effects through the system. The other arteries and capillaries try to compensate by opening up. So she's bleeding in a bunch of new different places, and it's a lot of work to get all of that straightened out.

"Finally, she gets out of surgery. She's still got a big hole in her abdomen. They stitched up the fascia, which is the muscle, but she's still got this big hole in her, packed with gauze. They're in the hospital for sixteen days. At last, we got her home. I've been handling it okay because I don't really have a choice. I've got these two people to care for, her and Flora. And Sally's dealing with it because she's got Flora to look after. She's still got that hole in her belly, and I'm changing those dressings every day. She's been doing good. Next week, they finally stitch her up."

With a huge, rough finger, he strokes his baby's cheek. "I don't care if you have the most boring life ever," he tells her. "Be an accountant. Be a geek. How you came into this world is enough excitement to last you a lifetime, my girl."

Belonging

BELLE BOGGS

I'm not from here. In the rural Virginia community where I grew up, that would matter—my parents' house, which they've owned for more than twenty years, is still known around our fifty-person town as "the Griggs house" (or, occasionally, "the annex," after its role as a space for extra hospital beds during the Civil War). Their neighbor Jimmy, an excellent gardener of zinnias and sunflowers, was born some eighty years ago in my parents' living room. Mrs. Walker, whose husband's family founded the town of Walkerton, is memorialized by her son through the meticulous upkeep of her years-empty house, right next door.

But here in the Triangle of North Carolina, it's common to be from elsewhere. In line at Harris Teeter, seniors with New York accents ask perplexed teenager cashiers why there aren't any rugelach in the bakery. Canvassing voters in Siler City, I talk to people from Florida, Mexico, Michigan, and Costa Rica, and I regularly meet neighbors who have barely changed their license plates. This phenomenon isn't confined to the Triangle, though it's probably especially pronounced here—North Carolina has an overall rate of in-migration and growth that far exceeds the national average. (It's no wonder, when every other week there's an article in the *New York Times* extolling our restaurants, music scene, and food trucks.) In the defunct 2006-era subdivisions near my house, you can still see signs in the weedy, empty lots welcoming Dr.-and-Mrs. so-and-sos from across the Northeast and Mid-Atlantic.

Some of my favorite local writers did not start their lives here either, but write about their adopted state with an ease that makes me a little jealous. My friend Marjorie Hudson—born in Illinois—writes, in her fine *Accidental Birds of the Carolinas*, about women who have found a home and respite here. Duncan Murrell, who grew up in Maryland, deftly chronicles life and death in Chatham County for national magazines like *Oxford American* and *Harper's*. Paul Cuadros moved here from D.C. to document immigration in Siler City and wound up coaching (and writing about) a championship-winning soccer team (of immigrants). Our last three poets laureate have been from Georgia, South Carolina, and Pennsylvania.

My husband and I arrived in Durham after years of apartment-hopping in Los Angles and Brooklyn. We chose the state deliberately. Richard went to school at Chapel Hill, so we knew plenty of people here already. North Carolina was cheap enough that I could take time away from teaching to write, and—at the time—was known in the South for its comparatively progressive politics. It wasn't too cold in the winter—that was something I'd never gotten used to in New York—and was the perfect distance from our families: close enough to get home in a few hours, but not so close that they might drop in. We bought a hand-built cabin in Chatham County, we got some kayaks and learned the best routes on the Haw. We imagined starting our own family here.

Though I have no intention of moving away, it's been harder for me to identify as a North Carolina writer. I wrote most of my first collection of short stories while living in Durham, but they're all set back home, in King William and King and Queen Counties. No matter how much time I spend on the stunning, rock-strewn Haw, "river" still means wide and flat, tidal, to me. I can't agree with my farmer friend's dismissal of the Hanover tomato as inferior to the heirlooms he grows in Hillsborough. A southern accent, in my mind, is still the soft and peculiar, slightly English-inflected Tidewater one. Other fiction I've written since my first collection was published— some short stories, and a novel—takes place in Virginia and

Florida, and only glancingly mention the state I now call home. This bothers me—I want to belong, to claim my place here—but if everyone I meet is here from somewhere else, then how am I really writing about North Carolina?

So I began, without realizing it, by writing about the state's original inhabitants, her animals: specifically the bald eagles, cormorants, deer, cicadas, and geese that surround my home in Chatham County. I wrote about them not in short stories but in essays considering nature and reproduction, at a time when I was fearful that I might never have children, or the life my husband and I imagined when we moved here. I also closely followed the stories of Jamani and Olympia, two female lowland gorillas in captivity at the North Carolina Zoo, both miraculously pregnant in the past few years (successful pregnancies in captive gorilla populations are rare), and the public clamoring over the births of their infants. Like me, like so many of my neighbors, Jamani and Olympia are migrants too, born in California and Georgia (and tracing their lineage back to the forests and swamps of central Africa), though Bomassa and Apollo, their young, will be solid North Carolinians.

I think writing about animals and nature helped connect me with my earliest experience of landscape, which must have influenced me to become a writer. When I was very young, before my family moved to Walkerton, we lived in more-isolated places along the Mattaponi River: in a rented house on a 2,600-acre soybean farm, then in a 100-year-old log cabin on a mill pond. There were always places to walk, wild enough that you could almost get lost. During deer season, a blaze orange vest was a necessity. I didn't live in a neighborhood with other kids, so it was usually just me and my brother, or me alone. We caught painted turtles from the lake, spotted bald eagles and wild geese in flight above the river. All that silence, walking, contemplation: it's part of what made me a writer.

I can remember my father pointing to a stretch of pine woods near our house and telling me, "That will all be gone when you grow up." I was stricken by his matter-of-fact pronouncement, though I realized that what he said must be true. So that also became a motivation for writing too: preserve what is there, because one day it will be gone. I recognize this same impulse in the students I meet, traveling across the state as a visiting artist for the North Carolina Arts Council. From Cherokee to Columbus Counties, they write about the same things: hunting land and forested thinking places gone to development, about muddy creeks and closed-down skating rinks. They write about what they already miss.

I still make almost daily treks to the Haw River; I spend a lot of time outside, and a lot of time alone. My hippie neighbors aren't big hunters (thank god), so there's no need for blaze orange, but sometimes, trespassing on someone else's property, I'm reminded of being a kid in Virginia: how far from home can I walk before dark? Is it possible to get lost? Soon I'll have the pleasure of seeing the landscape through my daughter's eyes, and I expect that the experience will deepen my sense of place, and probably the urgency I feel when I think of parts of it disappearing. I can imagine showing her the bald eagles' nest across from our spot on the Haw, taking her to visit our neighbors' goats, or maybe—if we're lucky— spying a bobcat and her kittens from our living room window.

Today I write both fiction and nonfiction, probably in equal measures, and I think both forms are suited to this drive for preservation. North Carolina has given me a lot to write about as an essayist and journalist—I've interviewed scientists and doctors about human and nonhuman infertility and reproduction, have traveled around the state to meet people involved in the fight for compensation for victims of forced sterilization—but I know what will really make me feel like a North Carolina writer. A new book of short stories.

There's something about the short story collection that requires the deepest kind of place knowledge. Think of *Dubliners* or *Lost in the City*; think of Jill McCorkle, Alan Gurganus, Randall Kenan, or Marjorie Hudson. For a long time, I didn't set my stories here—I didn't think I was qualified—but maybe that is changing. Recently, I was touring a house built by Bill Spiegel, who designed and built our cabin in the 1970s. He was hoping that Richard and I might one day decide to trade up (not likely), but I could also tell that he was proud of what he'd imagined and constructed: the huge, south-facing windows, the soaring ceilings and salvaged touches, the many decks and landings. We finally made it to the third and top floor—a giant master suite, with a bay window and a Jacuzzi.

"Wow, Bill," I said. "You lived here all alone?"

"Not *all* alone," he said. "I had female guests. Occasionally."

Walking home, I started thinking about all the people I've met in North Carolina who are truly of this place: Bill, the bachelor mayor of Chicken Bridge Road; my canvass buddy Jesse Scotton, who knows every street (and most of the people) in Siler City; Willis Lynch, who performs Jim Reeves songs Friday nights at the Norlina VFW; my adult education students in Durham, tackling the GED subject by subject. All those kids I met through the Arts Council: in Hiwassee Dam and Black Mountain, in Cerro Gordo and Yadkin County. And the newcomers, who have, after all, chosen this place. I won't write stories *about* them, of course—that isn't really how fiction works—but I can imagine pieces of these people creeping in to my next collection, which I have started to think will be set here.

And one more thing: you may have seen the *Time* magazine feature, "Which state suits you most?"—an online test (and procrastination device) that seeks to match respondents with the best state for their personality. A lot of my friends—even my husband, a committed Tar Heel—were matched with Georgia. I took the test twice. My results?

"You belong in North Carolina!"

I'm reading it as a sign.

No Man Nomad No More

STEPHANIE ELIZONDO GRIEST

The morning after my man called us quits—the one it took a decade to find, the one I loved and thought I might marry—I awoke with an almost violent sense of urgency. Not to call my girlfriends or a therapist. Not to pour another tequila. Not to scribble down all the reasons why we shouldn't break up so I could try to convince him otherwise when he returned home from work that evening.

No. My urgency was to find a job.

Not that I didn't already have one. I had been a travel writer for fifteen years by that point, a career that had whisked me to forty countries and birthed four books along the way. But while I was flush in "experience," I was broke in terms of assets: no car, no stocks, no bonds, no pension plan, no furniture that wasn't previously owned by a graduate student. I had an army of friends and a super-tight family, but they were scattered all over the world. At thirty-seven years old, I had no child, no cat, no potted plant—and suddenly now, no man.

Rolling out of his bed, I surveyed my options. June was just about over; in August, I'd be starting my final year at my MFA program in Iowa. I had flown to South Texas a few weeks prior so we could spend the summer together here in his condo, and had been assuming I'd move in for good once I graduated. Not only was I originally from the area, I was writing a book about it. But Texas wasn't big enough for both of us. I needed a new life plan.

Normally in situations like this, I cashed in some frequent flyer miles and bolted. But for the first time ever, there was no new country I was raring to visit, no faraway city I must explore. I wasn't even interested in alternative summer housing (which is why I was still occupying his condo, despite the detriment to dignity). After years of chasing stories around the globe, I just wanted to breathe instead of pant—preferably upon a chair that wasn't half duct tape, like all mine back in Iowa. I wanted a community of fellow writers and artists and students. I wanted a bed with a headboard. I wanted a dentist.

And for all of that, I needed a job.

Before I got online and started prowling, I drew up a few lists. The first one was:

Cities I'd Love To Live In
Austin!
New York!!
San Francisco
Albuquerque
Tucson
New Orleans

This was followed by:

Cities I Could Potentially Enjoy Living In,
    Especially for a Tenure-Track in My Genre
San Antonio
Anchorage
Chicago
Portland
Boulder
Seattle
Boston
D.C.
Philly

And finally:

Cities I Wouldn't Necessarily Slit My Wrists In
    (Unless I Was Teaching Freshman Comp)
Houston
St. Louis

Miami

Atlanta

Boise

Los Angeles (?)

Dallas (??)

This, I hoped, would keep me from applying for positions in, say, Buttzville, Mississippi, no matter how grave the situation became.

Before logging on to the first of many academic jobsites, I added Chapel Hill to the "love to live" list. I don't know why I did this. It was the only place on any list I had never visited. I didn't know if it was by the mountains or by the ocean, if it was a proper city or a college town or some glorified suburb of—Greensboro, was it? Somehow, I was drawn to it. Maybe because it sounded like a place where the banjo played, an instrument I'd adored since, well, Kermit in the *The Muppet Movie*. Maybe because it conjured images of magnolia trees proud and fragrant, of cornbread dripping in butter, of porches that wrapped around the whole block. Unfounded or not, these images landed Chapel Hill on my A-list.

Since it was still early summer, only a few positions had been posted that day, but one was at a university in New York City. That inspired me to spend the morning updating my CV. When my (ex-) man called to check on me, however, I suddenly remembered why I was doing so, and collapsed. For the remainder of that summer, I questioned every aspect of being. Surely my biological clock must be ticking: why couldn't I hear it? Wasn't reproduction the whole point of being human? Was I lying to myself that books and students could fill the void of blood?

Yet late at night, after he had fallen asleep beside me, I would sneak into his office and log onto the jobsites to see if anything new had been posted. In that dark quiet room, engulfed in MacBook glow, I wondered who I was meant to be: a writer/housewife or a writer/professor? Or should I just revert back to being a writer/nomad?

Since leaving my parents' house in Corpus Christi, Texas, at age eighteen, I have lived in the following locales: Austin, Seattle, Washington, D.C., Moscow, Beijing, El Paso, Brooklyn, three cities in Mexico, Princeton, Iowa City, and a remote village near the New York/Canada border. When I met the man in 2008, I was fully nomadic. Three-quarters of my possessions were stuffed in a storage shed in Manhattan while the rest were either physically on my person or at my parents' house in Texas. I hadn't slept in the same city for more than thirty consecutive nights in over two years. Books were my life then—researching them, writing them, promoting them—but each one generated only enough income to start the next; not enough for incidentals like rent and utilities. So I kept moving, from speaking gig to art colony, art colony to speaking gig, crashing with friends in the interim.

"Home" thus became a fluid concept, something other than an actual place. For a while it was an aesthetic: overstocked bookshelves, hardwood floors topped by Turkish carpets, spice jars with handwritten labels, a garden lovingly tended. Then it became a certain energy, the kind that emanated from taco stands run by little old viejitas calling you m'ija, or from food co-ops with so many flyers pinned to their bulletin boards, you couldn't see the cork. During my longer stints of nomadism, home became even more basic: anywhere I could boil a pot of rice milk, stir in some oats, and top with walnuts and blueberries in the morning.

After falling in love, home became a person. Sometimes he even said this to me: "You are home." Though I never knew exactly what he meant by this—if *I* was *his* home, or if I was home because his condo was our shared home and now I was back, or if we *both* were home simply by virtue of being together—it felt like the most romantic thing anyone had ever told me, as well as the most dangerous. If *he* was home, it could only mean I was homeless, now that we were through.

When I crossed the threshold of my Iowa apartment that August, my task was clear: I had nine months to write and defend a thesis, teach four classes, and, oh yes, chart the course of the rest of my life. I vowed to apply to three positions every Monday and to refrain from thinking about it the rest of the week, but I was stalking the jobsites before I'd even finished unpacking. Here were the options: Murray, Kentucky. Pocatello, Idaho. Dayton, Ohio. Ewing, New Jersey. Indianapolis. Cities I Wouldn't Necessarily Slit My Wrists In lengthened, while Cities I'd Love To Live In grew even more urgent: Cities I'd Slit Someone Else's Wrists To Live In.

Then one September morning, a new position appeared from the University of North Carolina–Chapel Hill. Not only was it a tenure track, it was in my genre, creative nonfiction—a combination only half a dozen universities in the nation were offering that year. I stared at the post for an extended minute, afraid to click on it lest it vanish like water on a fast-approaching highway. *It's probably a five-five teaching load, summers included. It's probably for writers who have published a dozen books in multiple genres.*

It wasn't.

Campus visits started a few months later. Soon I was flying from upstate New York to Seattle to Chicago to St. Louis to Boston to Miami, teaching classes, running workshops, giving readings, delivering pedagogy talks, chatting up perspective colleagues whose books I'd crammed on the plane. Though every job had its merits, I stalked Wiki for movement on the UNC position immediately afterward. For those who (enviably) don't know, Wiki is where academic job seekers anonymously post whatever correspondence they've had with a particular university, whether they've been invited to submit additional materials or heard a rumor that an "inside candidate" had all but signed the contract. Basically, Wiki is academic meth, only twice as addictive. Yet no one posted anything about Chapel Hill, not even when I typed "anyone know anything about this?" beneath it.

Then in late January, after a long day of teaching, I checked my phone messages to find one from the chair of UNC's English Department. My heart between my temples, I called her back. Within seconds, we were laughing. The chair of the Creative Writing Program, Daniel Wallace, picked me up from Raleigh-Durham International a week later. More laughter, followed by serious story swapping. The first place he took me was Weaver Street co-op in Carrboro. It was early February, but the sun was gold and the sky was blue. As we walked through the courtyard, I noticed a pair of overflowing bulletin boards. Inside was a Hot Bar featuring a fresh batch of cornbread, ready for buttering, and at checkout, the couple in front of us chatted in Spanish, my mother's tongue. After lunch, Daniel dropped me off at the Carolina Inn, which featured a mile-long porch, and as I headed toward the reception desk, a man walked by carrying a banjo case.

When I moved to North Carolina in July 2013, I owned the following furniture: a battered desk, a rusted filing cabinet, and a little red loveseat I had rescued from a clearance sale years before. Altogether, it filled half of one room in my new apartment. Furnishing the others induced a crisis of existential proportions.

Am I more likely to meet someone if I round up a bunch of crappy furniture, or if I invest in super nice furniture? Crappy furniture would sort of signal, hey, I'm not too set in my ways, I could easily merge paths with you, and I wouldn't think twice about hocking this stuff on Craigslist so we could go out and furnish our new home together. Super nice furniture, meanwhile, might say something like: look how responsible and tasteful I am. Even my end tables match. Why, if we joined paths, you'd just need to bring a change of clothes. I even have extra linens.

Wait a minute. Didn't Newsweek *once publish a report saying single, college-educated women over forty were more likely to die in a terrorist attack than walk down the aisle? If I'm destined to spend the rest of my life alone, I shouldn't hold back here.* Give me that La-Z-Boy, and the little ottoman too.

Two thousand dollars, delivery not included? *I could go to India for that. I could buy a pony. I don't need a La-Z-Boy.* Excuse me, where's the nearest Ikea? *Charlotte? Where the hell is that?*

Forget the chair. What I need is a bed. Here's a nice one, with a headboard and everything. Five hundred bucks. That seems reasonable. Here's my Master—excuse me? That's just for the headboard? Well, how much is the mattress?

!!

Could you point me to the futons?

A hundred bucks: that's more like it. I'll take two. Pardon? That's just for the cover? *This hideous pea-green cover?*

Wait. Is this the bed I am going to sleep in every night for the rest of my life? Or just until tenure? That's how they should categorize furniture in college towns: pre-tenure, post-tenure, no tenure. Compromise: I'll get a real bed, but hold off on the headboard. A mattress can just flop on the floor, can't it? Or is that the difference between being a writer/nomad and a writer/ professor: a bed with a headboard?

Dios mio. Here's my card. Charge it quick.

Although I haven't lived in Texas since the turn of the millennium, although I have never driven a truck or fired a pistol, although I despise its legislative stance on everything from abortion to fracking, I am rabidly Texan. My home state is the state of Molly Ivins and breakfast tacos, of salsa and Selena, of Ann Richards and accordions, of cowboy boots and Wendy Davis; of big hair, bigger personalities, and the biggest whoppers you ever heard; of roads so flat you could roll a bowling ball from Oklahoma to Mexico.

So when the North Carolina DMV demanded I "surrender" my Texas driver's license a mere seven days upon my arrival, a document that, at age sixteen, had been harder to earn than my high school diploma (having failed the driving test three times before a state trooper took pity and passed me), I panicked. *Surrender? As in, give it up? To you? But it's my identity. I hail from a hundred years of cowboys, mister. ¡Soy Tejana!*

Ditto with my New York State license plates. I know it's silly, but I wanted to keep them, as they attested to another key aspect of my identity. My soul might be Texan, but my wiring is pure New Yorker. When the DMV informed me that I must mail my plates back to the Empire State, I had another psychic meltdown. *Didn't you see how fast I marched up to this desk, sideswiping women and children? Do you have any idea how many little black dresses I own, or how uninhabitable I find anyplace without twenty-four-hour Cuban-Chinese take-out? Can't you hear how rapidly I am speaking to you? I'm pure New Yorker, baby!*

By mid-July, I had signed a North Carolina apartment lease, pension plan, I-9 form, W-2 form, and a pile of insurance papers; had acquired a North Carolinian dentist, physician, hairdresser, optometrist, mechanic, gynecologist, cable company, electric company, and water and sewer company; and had been issued a North Carolina State driver's license, voter registration card, library card, banking card, and co-op card. Within three weeks of my arrival, I was officially Carolinian, despite not knowing what that even meant.

And yet, and yet: after every angst-ridden errand ended, I got to drive past Weaver Street en route to my apartment in Carrboro—past the families sprawled across the lawn, chatting beneath the oak trees (or, in the case of an exceptionally lithe black man with a white goatee, dancing beneath the oak trees). For dinner, I could walk to a fleet of food trucks and order carne asada wrapped in a corn tortilla with a slice of lime from a lady from Michoacán and then plunk down among gente from Jalisco to eat it. I could stroll through the woods afterward, the trail ablaze with fireflies, and sip wine on my deck while the cicadas made their awesome racket, then roll out of bed the following morning for a yoga class and maybe swing by the farmer's market for an heirloom tomato the size of my head.

I used to fantasize about a life like this when traveling wore me down. Like that night I passed in a hospital in Oaxaca after amoebas detonated my digestive tract. Lying there all alone, watching an IV drip into my wrist while my mother back in Texas tried to determine whether the medical insurance I had bought on the Internet would cover it, an unprecedented thought popped into my brain: this shit is getting old.

And then: *I* am getting old.

And finally, resignedly: *I* am getting too *old* for this *shit*.

North Carolina promised a calmer life, a nourishing life, one that would restore instead of deplete. And also delight: every day, it seemed, I found a new source of happiness. The way men young and old called me "Ma'am" and women called me "Honey." The way any patch of green was good enough for a garden, and the way each plant wore a little name tag. The way waitresses always asked if I wanted grits or biscuits with that. The way strangers parted on the bus: "You have yo'self a good day now!" The fried catfish on the breakfast menu and the fried green tomatoes on the dinner menu. The mammoth butterflies delicately sipping nectar. The abundance of bike trails. The hand-plucked music that spilled from backyards and garages and porches. The deer that, when you stood still, emerged from the trees. The stories and the laughter that inspired even more stories.

One morning, I woke up worrying this state might make me a little *too* soft, that I'd lose my urban edge. I like to write about things like drug trafficking and human smuggling: where do butterflies fit in that? But then I tuned in WUNC and discovered I could get arrested at the capital that very afternoon if I wanted, along with hundreds of others at the weekly Moral Monday demonstrations. I logged onto Facebook and saw that I could caravan up to Washington for the 50th anniversary of Dr. Martin Luther King's historic march, or—if that wasn't possible—participate in one of thirteen rallies being held across the state. From there I followed links to the North Carolina Justice Center, the Durham Immigrant Solidarity Committee, and El Pueblo. Before I knew it, my fingers had curled into note-taking position.

As a travel writer, place is my chief muse—its legends, its issues, its people. Yet I have never written about a place while still a resident of it. I wrote my first book, a travel memoir about Russia, China, and Cuba, while ensconced in my childhood bedroom in Texas. My Mexico memoir sprung from a succession of art colonies in New York, Nebraska, Arkansas, and Texas. I started a book about silence in Barcelona, and another about the Texas/Mexico borderland while roaming around the New York/Canada borderland.

Part of the reason is circumstantial: as someone who constantly changes locations but writes at a glacial pace, I simply never catch up to writing about where I actually am. I take mad notes, reams of them, while my boots are on the ground, but I don't spin them into stories until I'm thousands of miles away. I have come to relish the distance this system brings, as it enables me to make sense of the particular time I spent in the particular place. Otherwise, I'd probably step onto the street each morning and realize everything I had written the night before was wrong.

Yet I could be living in North Carolina for years to come. Decades, even. Nomadism could be ending right here, right now, and while I find this terrifying, it is also immensely relieving. Because when I think back to that awful morning that precipitated this move, I realize that my compulsion wasn't just to find a source of income, but to find a source of home. And while I still haven't figured out what this home will ultimately look like—whether I'll fill it with a man and children or pets and plants or maybe just books and me—I am profoundly grateful to have a home (and a bed with a headboard) of my own in such a magical place.

So here I am, one month into my Carolinian adventure, the first place I've ever visited without a return ticket. What stories will I find here; which scenes will I re-create? Time to step out and find out.

Five Encounters with Vegetation

WILL BLYTHE

THE WOODS

The August night tells me that I'm home once again, down from New York City, where I've lived since 1987, a long barreling interstate drive away. In the garage, the Subaru's cooling engine ticks and clatters. All around me as I stretch and unbend, the darkness of a Chapel Hill neighborhood resounds, a vast, pulsing rave of cicadas, crickets, and frogs, with the occasional hoot of an owl thrown in to terrify the small mammals. If you saw me then, you'd witness a man on the far end of middle age, standing in his mother's driveway, listening intently for something he can't quite hear, despite the loudness of the insect clamor. He's in no hurry to go inside, though his mother, half-asleep on the couch, waits up for him just as she did when he was in high school. Within two or three months she will be driven to the hospital and never come home again.

He just stands there, listening, soaking in the reverberant waves of noise, as if this time, after all these years, he might decipher the night's impenetrable code, as if a meaning lurks there just beyond his ken.

The feeling is similar to when I was a boy and I hovered in the grass of my grandparents' lawn in Huntersville, North Carolina, eavesdropping on the adults who sat on the patio, speaking in low, comfortable voices mingled with the occasional shrieking laugh (like those owls), ice chiming in their glasses of tea. Maybe my father and my uncle were drinking something a little stronger. Probably they were.

Judge Phillips, a friend of ours, says he knew he was home

from the Second World War, where he saw terrible things, when the train taking him south pulled into little hamlets and he heard at long last the drone of the cicadas. Let's admit that this sound has been a longtime staple of southern comfort, and not just for the Judge.

And yet sometimes when I wake up in the middle of the night, the roaring in the vegetation is not so much soothing as it is infernal, a manic, electrified buzzing, an unstinting cacophony that won't shut the hell up. That drone reminds me of how inhuman nature can be, how little it cares for us despite our toasty maternal fantasies of it, a conclusion that even the great nature lover Henry David Thoreau came to when he ascended the barren alpine heights of Maine's Mount Katahdin and nearly went mad from the terror of implacable ice and rock. The gentle shore of Walden Pond was galaxies away. Here was infinity, here was man. The two did not go together.

A fellow in such a state comes to realize that his own mind is at once a part of this clamorous, dissolving madness and yet distinct from it. And there is no comfort in either position. If God is present in the insect roar and the icy altitudes, it is an infernal God, the God of Absence and Accident, the God of Hurricanes and Whirlwinds, of Asteroids and Black Holes and Dwarf Stars, of Plane Crashes and Birth Defects and Random Acts of Violence, of Crocodiles and Snakes, the God of Being Picked Randomly Out of a Line for Execution.

I have always wished for an exception, a loophole out of which one might climb above mortal fear. The summer I was fourteen, I dreamed that a Majestic Joyous Presence was awaiting me outside on the front porch of my parents' house. In an ecstasy of anticipation, I wrapped the bedclothes around me, thinking they were a royal robe, and for the first and only time of which I am aware, sleepwalked up the stairs and opened the front door to meet the Majestic Joyous Presence. The streetlamp buzzed. The cicadas roared. No one was there. Still asleep, I wept on the front porch.

Then I went back downstairs, the bedclothes dragging behind me, a solitary, jilted king returning to bed.

Yet I keep listening for something. Sometimes at noon down south on the hottest of days, when everyone is shivering inside their Arctic offices, I go outside by myself just to hear the metallic whirring of the cicadas start up in the trees on the edge of a parking lot. The cicadas' tymbals pulsate against their abdomens and the thick air reverberates with the loneliest sound in the universe.

For some reason, I am drawn to that sound the way some men are drawn to fuck up their happy lives. There's no good reason for this. It's simply who we are. We're bound to be alone.

The South in general and North Carolina in particular offer up at least a dozen standard-issue muses, a dozen rationales for writers to exercise their tymbals against their abdomens and generate an unholy racket in the weeds. The list is as familiar and belated as a great aunt's recipe for ambrosia. There is the instigating subject of "family," though there have been known to be families elsewhere. Somewhat linked together, there is the "War Between the States," the "original sin of slavery," and the "land"—"the land, Beauregard, the land!" There is also the "Christ-haunted landscape," lest we forget dear sweet Jesus.

And yet my muse is none of these things exactly, substantial though they all may be. Mine is the roaring blankness embodied in an August night, mine is the South as the place that refuses to tell all that it knows. Mine is the transit point between the awesomely inhuman and the familiarly local, between the dead and the living. Mine is the silence that wishes to be said. Mine is nothing at all.

A BOXWOOD

One summer many years ago, M. and I took mushrooms at the family farm. "Are you sure this isn't going to make them less potent?" M. asked as I brewed up a psilocybin tea. We had come south from New York City for a "working vacation." M. liked his drugs. He'd done ayahuasca the previous year even though it left him shaking in the felicitously named Cosmic Coffee Shop at Broadway and 58th when I met him the next day.

"No worries," I said. "This is a tried and true technique." In truth, I was secretly hoping the tea might not be all that potent, having myself not long before endured a twenty-four-hour nightmare produced by doctored hashish that in its evil thrall had me repeating to anyone who would listen (including my boss), "I just want to wake up into the dream that is my life."

In the recent context, potent was worrisome. Potent had a way of turning New York City into an alien space craft. Potent had me start drinking a glass of water and become terrified that the water in the glass was endless. Potent had me hiding behind the door from the managing editor, who would not have understood the trouble that bored young men can get into on a Wednesday afternoon. Potent had me asking my wife to say something that I didn't expect her to say so that I would know she was not a figment of my imagination. I didn't know what Potent would do down south.

When the tea took effect, quite kindly as it turned out, M. and I lay together with our heads under the sofa so that the darkness of that location might accentuate the patterns appearing in the exact same order (paisleys, spirals, lightning bolts) on the inside of our eyelids. We giggled at the possibility that we might be discovered with our heads under a couch while engaged in this investigation.

After a while, I left M. to the multiplex of his eyelids and wandered outside into an afternoon saturated with greenery and was led for reasons unknown to sit in the presence of a lovely boxwood which sparkled before me like a voluptuous, unkempt, green brain that had the power of telepathy. Bees were zigging and zagging into and out of the bush, as if bringing communiques to the central nervous system. All the yard was wired together with light. And there before me was the boxwood, which seemed to be saying in its vegetative language that *everything is as it is.* Which is another way of saying: *This is it.* Meaning (in the Carolinian vernacular): *This right here is all there is.*

Mind you, Moses himself listened to a bush.

For southern Christians, raised as we have been to see the world in front of us as mere staging for the next life, the boxwood's sentiments came as a necessary correction. Like something William Blake would have said had William Blake been a telepathic bush. This world is all there is and yet it is enough. More than enough. The afternoon vibrated to an unheard, joyous music.

For a while longer, I sat there at peace. The mushrooms were polite, as befits a proper southern shroom. I had a sense of an ample life force pulsing through this old beaten yard where normally I might have parked the car and gone onto the porch without a second thought.

When I finally started coming down, I went back inside the house, where M. was watching the Olympics on a tiny TV. We talked a little bit about how God is felt to be everywhere in the South, how in that sense you don't have a lot of privacy. But then you're never really alone, either. There's always Someone with Whom to Have a Conversation, even if it's a little one-sided, which most people don't really mind, as long as it's their side that gets the airing. Then M. said, "Man, this TV is really tiny." Which was not a drug perception. It was a tiny TV. And so we welcomed back the mundane.

In the years since, the boxwood seems to have disappeared during a bout of landscaping. The grass stretches lushly towards the field where we once ran cattle.

POTATOES

She liked to laugh at me in a way that drove me insane.

I didn't know what thread count was, for instance. And apparently, I had mistaken sheets with artificial fibers for pure cotton sheets. This proved I was a rube. She told me about New York, design, Knoll Associates, where she worked, a Japanese boyfriend who tried hard to please her. She told me that if I came to New York not to live in the East Village like everyone else who came to New York in those days.

I bridled against such glamorous injunctions.

On the advice of our mutual friend, she had sent me her poetry months before when I was living down in Alabama. I had long admired her from a distance. I wrote her that her poems lacked nouns. I was wrong, but I didn't know that then. She herself was a succession of lovely nouns, some proper, some not. She had been a dancer and she was proud of her body.

Despite my authoritative lessons on poetry, the poems kept coming. And in between my decrees about nouns, we began to make little confessions about ourselves. What we liked. What we did that day. Did I mention that I had a girlfriend? I probably surrounded the notion with inviting ambiguity.

She said if I came to New York on a visit, to call her. I called her from an icy street in early January. She seemed not to be in. I left a message and went home, more than a thousand miles to Alabama. She wrote me a letter in return, telling me she was disappointed I didn't have more of a southern accent. I could have accentuated mine as naturally happened around family, but I balked. She was maddening. That wicked laugh of hers. As if she knew something about me that I did not know about myself. A year or so later, I threw her out of my room one night. The memory still makes me happy and shames me, all at once.

More nouns, I told her as the poems continued to arrive. Every romance needs resistance—obstacles that you can look back on knowingly, wondrously, as you lie next to each other at the time of your first mutual confession. *When did you know...* Her mockery. My rules. Insufficiencies against which to labor. A plot.

We met the next summer at her friend's apartment in Chapel Hill. I had moved back to North Carolina for a spell between jobs. Her friend's black lace underwear was pinned to the clothesline on the balcony. I proposed a swim in the complex's pool. We swam in our underwear during a violent, early evening thunderstorm, lightning illuminating our faces as if we were suspects being photographed. I remember laughing exultantly, like a drunk. What kind of death would this be, a fool splashing through a field of lightning? Clearly, I was willing to die an idiot's death in pursuit of her.

I invited her to come visit me later that summer in the country. On her first night there is when she told me about New York and design and how these weren't real cotton sheets. I gave her a room of her own, which is somehow where I ended up under some ridiculous guise having to do with ghosts in the house.

We stayed up all night. She asked me if I loved her. She was such a cosmopolitan person, I was surprised at the question. I probably hedged in some unconscionable way. Though if I didn't exactly love her like that, I did love that moment and she was in it, in the near-dawn in the second-floor bedroom on artificial sheets. Pursuit has something amoral in it, the thrum of possibility, the hunger for trying on a new life, if only for a day.

In the field outside, just below the bedroom window, the neighbors were digging potatoes that morning. They called me to join them. With my bare feet sinking into the dirt, I thought of her back in the bedroom waiting for me and wondered: What will she look like? What will she say? How will it be different this time?

That was in the days when I thought I knew what the muse demanded. Nouns, more nouns.

If it were only that simple.

MAGNOLIAS, GRASS

It was my mother who told me that I, too, would have to die one day. I was four or five, standing beside her in the backyard of the house we rented on McCauley Street as she put out the trash. This was probably no more than half a mile from the room in which she would die decades later at the UNC Medical Center.

There is a place as real as this moment where we will one day die, you who read this now, and me. I think about this every day, though I cannot for the life of me understand what it means. Contemplating death is guaranteed to melt the mind into a puddle of wax as if it were a candle.

I once visited Susan Sontag at her apartment in the London Terrace complex in New York. The cancer that would one day kill her had not yet recurred. Books were everywhere, even on top of the kitchen stove. For hours we sat at her kitchen table and talked about our favorite novels and writers. Her gusto was palpable. I think that she believed that she would live forever as long as there were more books to read. I cannot help but feel the same.

"Do I *have* to die?" I asked my mother in exactly the same way I might have asked "Do I *have* to go to bed?" I don't know why the subject of death had come up, some kid had probably told me about it, but already I was looking for the loophole. I should have become a lawyer. Many people have told me that over the years, including my ex-wife.

"Yes," my mother said. "We all have to die. But you don't have to worry about that for a long time."

She was being tender, I suppose, trying in the way of most mothers to allay my fears by putting off the moment of reckoning far into the distance. She was good at that. She herself would die not having visited a doctor for at least thirty or so years. Living with one for a good part of that time doesn't count. He didn't like to visit doctors, either.

"I don't want to have to worry about it," I said.

Prior to the age of five or so, I worried about things. At one point, I thought I was having a heart attack in the bathtub. I had seen a public service announcement from the American Heart Association on TV. I had all the advertised symptoms:

pain in my chest, shortness of breath, profuse sweating. "I'm having a heart attack," I said, summoning my parents to say goodbye.

"What makes you say that, Willie?" my father asked. My parents stood over the tub as I forlornly let the washcloth sink to the bottom. There was no need to scrub any longer. I was going to die. I recounted the symptoms. "I think it's gas, son," he said quite tenderly, grinning at my mother.

"I am not going to die," I told her that day in the backyard. I was angry. I felt as if my mother had the power to prevent my death. That all she had to do was say that I wouldn't die and then I wouldn't.

"Everybody dies," she said, the way mothers now say "everybody poops." Death, it appears, is the greatest democracy of them all. "But I'm telling you, you don't need to worry about it, not for a long, long time." The rhythms of her sentence turned it into a little lullaby, the "long, long time" part especially. But that was as much soothing as she was going to do that day.

As it turned out, she didn't like the fact that she was going to die, either. And as she was already in her thirties, she had a big head start on me in dying. So her "long, long time" was not quite as "long, long" as mine—in an instant, I was calculating the odds, an amateur at mortality tables and yet I knew I was likely in a better place than her. And I'm ashamed to say (though nothing could be truer) that I exulted even then at my presumed distance from the end. I would live alone on the earth if I had to—this I understood in an instant. The rest of humanity might have to go charging off a cliff into oblivion. I would stay back and watch everybody disappear, even my loved ones.

"It's not true," I said. "I'm not going to die. I'm not! I won't!"

My mother simply said "that's enough!" to all my whining and went inside to fix supper. I wandered off into the green, blooming backyards of McCauley and Ransom Streets and proceeded to forget about death for a while. I knew every tree, every shrub, every dog bone, every bird's nest, every board of every fence. I knew what the yards smelled like when a thunderstorm approached and the air crackled with ozone and the ladies raced into the yards to take down the laundry off the lines. I knew what the dirt smelled like after the rain. I knew how many years could pass on a single desultory morning where I would walk around prodding things with a stick until my father yelled, "Willie, stop messing with that dadgum stick!"

I had been banned from bringing sticks into the house. I did love them, sticks. They became what I wished in my hands—snakes, rifles, shovels, wands. That a stick in a Carolinian yard can become what you wish it—that's the first miracle, isn't it? That's making poetry before you even know what poetry is. A single stick in the right hands is a muse.

It had been lovely, my life as a young mammal in the days before death existed. Getting up before the rest of the household, eating the dog's food (the Purina as crunchy as breakfast cereal), stalking through the yard in the dewey mornings, hunting for fairies. They were there, I was sure, most likely in the flowers. I had read about them. Now I wanted to see one.

An eternity existed in every day. Trees, birds, insects. Even boredom was delirious. My sister Annie and I climbed the magnolia that stood outside the kitchen window, often plummeting to the ground when the branches snapped. We learned that we could survive having the wind knocked out of us as we lay there breathless on the hardpacked dirt at the base of the tree.

At night we caught lightning bugs between our hands and jailed them in Hellman's mayonnaise jars with holes punched in the lids. To our bedroom we took those jars containing an entire night sky of insect stars and comets and planets blinking peacefully and watched them as we fell asleep in our little beds. In the morning, the lightning bugs were almost always gone, having escaped through the air holes in the lid.

I found dog skulls in the corners of the yards, where old

mutts had crept in to die in private. I held them up and watched the wind blow through the spaces in the bone. The light arrowed through as well and hurt my eyes. The grass grew thick where things had died.

"Don't be messing with those bones," Louise, our housekeeper and my other mother, said. "They're dirty."

I poured the dirt out of the skull. "Not anymore," I told her. This was life before death.

A PINE AND AN OAK

Decades later, we buried my mother at the end of October in the Old Chapel Hill Cemetery in the same grave in which my father already lay, under a pine and an oak, where the headstone still had a blank space on its granite face awaiting her name and dates.

Her four children wrote the obituary together, all of us older than my mother was that distant day beside the trash cans when I discovered death. What I learned makes no more sense now than it did then.

"Nothing can happen nowhere," declared the Anglo-Irish writer Elizabeth Bowen as a justification for why setting in fiction matters. Hers is an attitude long considered sympathetic towards the southern enshrinement of place. I hear her words differently (and so might Samuel Beckett), so that two seemingly incompatible things are true at once: nothing, whatever nothing might be, comes into the world, and where that nothing happens is a place known (for lack of more precise words) as "nowhere." For me, that's where the cicadas sing from on a summer night—an emptiness that feels immense. Death, too, is nothing, and that's the good and the bad of it.

At the end of the graveside service, we touched the coffin and spoke our quiet farewells for the long voyage ahead. Without conferring, each of us reached down and picked up pine cones and placed them on the headstone in my mother's honor.

The months pass, and from time to time, the wind blows them off and we put them back. And then the wind blows them off again. And the next time we visit we put the pinecones back again.

I want to inscribe the blankness. Instead of the word made flesh, I'll settle for the flesh made word.

How hard it is to say goodbye. I know that nothing eventually gets the last word. I know that one day even the last word will disappear. But as I said, and will say again, we put the pinecones back.

Gloria Blythe
March 27, 1928–October 27, 2013

The Capital of Normal

MARIANNE GINGHER

Greensboro, North Carolina, dubbed the Gate City. Greens-*boring* we teenagers called the place. Grimsboro. Gate to *no-*where. I didn't know anybody whose dream was to stay. There wasn't anything wrong with the place, it was just such a *normal* town. Normal was like *average* and average meant C and C meant dumb. If you lived in Greensboro you were properly called a Greensburgher—how stupid-sounding was that?

I grew up in this mostly placid, Chamber of Commerce–picturesque piedmont town in a comfortable house in the leafy suburbs. Go ahead and hate me, you folks who were raised by rabid wolves, but my mother's name was Snow White and Prince Charming was my dad. I took piano lessons, owned a horse. I rode the horse all over Greensboro, back when there were barns with haylofts on Westridge Road, when Friendly Road was two narrow lanes, and Shoppes at Friendly (which today is home to a glossy Apple store, Anthropologie, Whole Foods) was a mammoth pasture. I didn't think about being a privileged southern white girl any more than I thought about breathing. It took the civil rights movement, beginning with the famous Woolworth sit-ins by local A&T University students, to cast a significant pall over my little corner of Elm Street and wake me up to the true grief in my land. Before that I had to manufacture my grief, which I was pretty good at. Throughout my adolescence, I affected a whiny bleakness—who knows why? Because I never made cheerleader? Maybe those of us who list in the direction of the artist's life simply know bone-deep that nothing worth having should come to us easily. If we have it too good, we're compelled to agitate, to mess it up. I knew early that I wanted to be a writer and writers' lives were troubled, fraught with debt, consumption, and drink. At fifteen I had no clue about trouble and I had no clue about who I was except that I was miserable. It didn't matter, all my advantages. None of it added up to peace of heart. It's what I didn't have that mattered: popularity, a straight-A brain, a boyfriend.

1963 was a very bad year for me at Grimsley High School in Greensboro, N.C. In the flattest shoes possible I was hurtling towards six feet tall. I weighed 117 pounds. I wore Liqui-mat make-up, an acne cover-up that looked like paste made from Calamine lotion and cement. My stringy blonde hair was struggling to grow out of the Prince Valiant cut of my younger days. I wanted hair like Peter, Paul and Mary's Mary Travers—long, straight, luminous corn-silk hair. I was a dreamy, lovesick girl without a boyfriend, besotted with poetry, and obsessed with Hester Prynne. I couldn't stop rereading *The Scarlet Letter*. It seemed the essential guide to suffering with dignity and going it alone without a man. I should have counted my blessings: maybe I was a social loser, but at least the pastor at the Presbyterian church my family attended hadn't gotten me with child.

America was seething with unrest. A bomb planted in a Birmingham, Alabama, church had killed four black girls earlier that year; thousands of people across the South were arrested during civil rights demonstrations. Martin Luther King was jailed in Birmingham after police unleashed dogs and used fire hoses and cattle prods against him and his supporters, including schoolchildren. My favorite poet, Robert Frost, died that year. Then, in November, my algebra teacher handed me back a quiz on which I'd scored yet another F just as the principal came on the PA and announced that President Kennedy had been shot. It's hard, even now, to remember a more distraught time in modern American history.

Most afternoons after school, I sequestered myself in my

bedroom to brood, write sonnets, and, when I wasn't paging through *The Scarlet Letter* seeking guidance, to listen to the radio. The Beatles' "I Wanna Hold Your Hand" was a huge hit, along with tunes by Little Stevie Wonder, the Beach Boys, Skeeter Davis, Martha and the Vandellas, and the Chiffons, all delivering the kind of feverish up-tempo love songs that made romance seem larky. Only Jimmy Gilmer and the Fireballs pounding out "Sugar Shack" on every station I dialed in tempted me to hurl myself out a window. I hated "Sugar Shack." It made me think of all the sugar I was never going to get. But in the wake of national heartbreak and upheaval, folk music flourished, and I listened and lapped up its antidote. Earnest songs about social injustice and the travail of martyrs and underdogs thrilled me. Finally people were singing about the ornery other stuff of life beyond the sinkhole of longing for love. Some grit in the sugar bowl.

In the adjacent bedroom my younger brother Knothead was practicing his guitar, a light blonde Espana he'd gotten for his thirteenth birthday. I could smell the cigarettes he and his pal Richard Newby were sneaking behind the locked door. Knothead was in the eighth grade, a smoky little hotdog looking to get laid. He'd determined that playing guitar would make him irresistibly layable, and most afternoons after school, when normally he'd have been beating up on a younger sibling or igniting his farts with the Zippo he'd stolen from Daddy, he practiced guitar until his fingers bled. Lately, he'd been drenching himself in Canoe cologne, and getting up early to iron his madras slacks before school and polish his tasseled Nettleton's. "Shout! Shout! (Knock Yourself Out!)" had been his favorite song, but, since his interest in girls, he preferred soulful acoustic ballads by the Kingston Trio, Joni Mitchell, Bob Dylan, and Joan Baez. His voice had changed, but it was croaky and still splintered, so he played safe and sung the melody high. Every now and then I heard Richard join in. I couldn't resist humming a little harmony in a lower octave—was my voice actually deeper than theirs? They heard me through the wall and stopped.

"Mom?"

I identified myself as not-Mom and, relieved, they opened the door and offered to teach me to inhale cigarettes if I wanted to learn. But when Knothead started strumming "Puff the Magic Dragon," we forgot about our cigarettes, fell into rapturous singing like a trio of drunks. Our eyes widened with every buttery note. We actually *blended*! Standing in the center of our threesome, our voices braiding, I felt as giddy as a Maypole. We sounded *good*, accidental virtuosos!

January 1964, a new year, a fresh start at last, one week before the Mid-Winter's Dance, Buddy Burton, the shortest boy in my class, called to invite me. I'd seen him at football games with other girls, all of them taller than Buddy (a fungus was taller than Buddy), sitting miserably in front of him, on a lower bleacher, to even out disparities in height when, as a couple, they stood up to cheer. What would happen at a dance, *without* bleachers?

There was no way to compensate him unless I went in a wheelchair.

"Let me know by tomorrow," he said. "The Bel-Tones Five are playing."

I hated the Bel-Tones Five, a group of smarmy college guys with crew cuts and gleaming Bible salesmen smiles. They wore yellow alpaca sweaters and Weejuns without socks. They sung sappy Lettermen and Johnny Mathis songs. I foresaw one slow dance after another, partnered with a boy the size of a mushroom.

When I arrived late for practice at Richard Newby's house, the ashtray on the living room coffee table already overflowed with butts. They hadn't practiced a lick, except French inhaling and blowing smoke rings, but they had big news. Knothead had wrangled us a first gig Saturday night at Mayfair's Suburban Family Restaurant in Friendly Shopping Center.

"*This* Saturday night?" I cried. It was a miracle. I would not have to be Buddy Burton's Attack of the Gargantuan Woman date. "Sorry, Buddy," I heard myself telling him, "but, after checking my busy calendar, I see that our folk trio has an engagement." I would have to practice saying it to believe it myself.

"What's the name of our group? We don't even have a name yet!" But I was ecstatic. "We've got to practice!"

They hated to practice, but we ran through a few numbers: "If I Had a Hammer," "Blowin' in the Wind," "The Sloop John B," "Greenback Dollar," "Oh, Mary, Don't You Weep, Don't You Mourn," and "Cotton Fields." I beseeched them to eliminate the silly verses they'd written for "Titanic": "Uncles and aunts, little children lost their pants"; "Small boys and girls, all went down in frothy swirls"; and "Grandma and Gramps swam real hard, got killer cramps." I worried that in the era of protest songs, making fun of tragedy—no matter that there were few people left alive to remember it—was in terrible, heartless taste. But the guys thought the goofy lyrics would be crowd pleasers and stuck them in.

When he wasn't practicing guitar after school, Knothead prowled the Friendly Shopping Center. Friendly was the first modern shopping center to be built near our neighborhood. It had opened when I was in junior high and Knothead, fifth grade. It was close enough so that you could ride your bike there. But my brother, even as a cool eighth grader now, often preferred to ditch his bike near the opening of a storm-water culvert on Edgewater Drive near Friendly Road and travel underground the quarter mile or so until he popped up from a curbside drain in front of Eckerd's drugstore. He and his pals could smoke in the culvert to their heart's content without threat of an intervening adult. Whenever she didn't have cheerleading practice, Debbie Clemmons (the most beautiful girl in seventh grade) joined Knothead in a booth at Jay's Delicatessen, where, after a slug or two of Binaca to freshen his breath, he courted her with all his snaky charm.

On one of his sojourns he'd run into Captain Coffee, a flamboyant, mustachioed barrel of a man who headed up the public relations office for the shopping center. The Captain's office walls were covered in autographed publicity shots of celebrities he'd glad-handed or known during or after his vaudevillian days: Ed Sullivan, Jack Benny, Milton Berle, George and Gracie Burns. There was even a picture of Jimmy Dodd, the grown-up leader of the Mouseketeers. Knothead, who had never met a stranger in his life and possessed a foghorn's bravado, was Captain Coffee's kind of guy: a kindred huckster spirit. Between them they had cooked up the Mayfair Restaurant debut and agreed that the Captain would act as our talent and booking agent.

At the eleventh hour, Mom came up with the name for our group: Two Thorns and a Rose. It didn't matter that, when my brother introduced us, he made a joke about being "the rose." I knew who the rose was supposed to be.

That Saturday we sang at the Mayfair Suburban Family Restaurant. There was candlelight. People put down their knives and forks to applaud. Our harmonies seemed to brocade the air long after our songs were finished. We'd stumbled into a place that thrummed with connection and reward. We had no words for it, but we could feel it: the satisfactions of art purring within and against us, playfully seductive, before we were ready for it, before we knew what art was or what to do with it. My heart felt like a sparkler. I was not at the Mid-Winter's Dance with tiny Buddy. I was part of a hit folk singing trio in which I was billed as the Rose.

Captain Coffee made sure we were photographed and written up in the *Greensboro Record*: three suburban teenagers dressed like Perry Como in matching V-neck sweaters, our mouths frozen in phony expressions of earnest mournfulness that singing protest songs without the experience of protest

MARIANNE GINGHER

142

gave us. My hair had not grown out; I still looked like Prince Valiant. You couldn't tell by the photo that I did my best to swing my pageboy as if it were Mary Travers's long bright corn-silk hair. But I did.

Many engagements followed, including a hootenanny benefit for the Heart Association and a political fund-raiser concert for "Skipper" Bowles, a Democrat running for governor who lost. We might have stayed singing together forever had not Captain Coffee asked us to perform at the Midget Convention.

"I can't do it," I said. "I *won't*."

"Why not?" Knothead howled. "We'd get to skip school that day."

"LOOK AT ME!" I shouted. "GET OUT THE MEASURING TAPE!"

"But we'd get *paid*," Richard said.

Of course I said no, not only because I was too tall to sing for midgets without feeling vastly embarrassed for us all, the inequity, the injustice, but because I wasn't yet grown up enough to reckon with the personal sacrifice and daring that art frequently demands. What I've come to believe over the years is that creative acts of any consequence begin with the artist forgetting about herself, and I wasn't there yet and wouldn't be for a long time to come.

After we turned down the Midget Convention, Captain Coffee viewed us as a group of callow pretenders not willing to suffer much for art, and he dropped us. It's true that we didn't suffer, nor did we ever make a dime. But that wasn't the point.

What *was* the point? For me, it was the feeling as we stood in the spotlight singing, of *accord*—that snug crux of harmony—all dissonance resolved, all fires put out, peace not protest. I simply couldn't sing and simultaneously long for something better. The singing *was* the better. Casting my voice over a spellbound audience, I accepted my good fortune and was not ashamed to exult in it and to imagine I was brightening the world.

The desire to create something brighter than myself, more generous, less picayune and vain, something which abates misery is what's guided my entire writing life, too. I learned it right there in my hometown, the Capital of Normal. Years later, in two memoirs, *A Girl's Life* and *Adventures in Pen Land*, I would credit both my functional family and the teachers who pried open the two-ton lid on my ignorance (all of those teachers resided in Greensboro, including my grad school mentor, Fred Chappell). And I would begin to believe that staying where one's imagination and earliest creative impulses arose and continued to flourish was neither shameful nor something that required apology. Might I even begin to call myself lucky?

As an adult, after sojourns in Winston-Salem and Chapel Hill, I ended up settling in Greensboro, raising my children there, writing my books. But I would never claim that it was the end of risk. Eudora Welty wrote that "a sheltered life can be a daring life as well, for all serious daring starts from within." And that's the mantra I comfort myself with whenever I feel that I missed out by not aiming myself towards the bright lights and big cities of elsewhere.

Long live Greensboro, land of shopping centers, suburban sprawl, a spindly downtown that's forever trying to reinvent itself, Guilford Battleground, colonial hero Nathanael Greene, birthplace of O. Henry with his cheesy trick endings, a baseball team called the Greensboro Grasshoppers—how corny is that?—a pretty downtown library, a glorious symphony orchestra, a magnificently restored train depot, the glossy Civil Rights Museum in the renovated Woolworth's—site of the original sit-ins in 1960—five four-year colleges, my old refurbished high school, more than 100 years old, where once, hardly realizing the privilege, I took an elective course, taught by Mrs. Mims, in which we read all the comedies and historical plays of Shakespeare. *All* of them. Who reads *Timons of Athens, Coriolanus,* and *Henry the IV* (Parts I and II) in high school anymore? Middling in size, well-intentioned, rarely newsworthy (there *was* the Klan vs. Communist Workers Party shootout back in the early 1980s) Greensboro, North Carolina: a place of harmony, unrest, heartbreak, longing, boredom, hypocrisy, kindness, injustice, saints, blowhards, noisemakers, creators and destroyers, givers, takers, peacemakers, agitators, philanthropists, do-gooders, the homegrown and the homeless, visionaries, fools, and dreamers— same as any place, and just enough different, too.

Diary, 2008–2013

ROSECRANS BALDWIN

1. Right around the time everything went to shit, John Edwards moved from his estate on Jones Ferry Road to a loft downtown in Greenbridge, to lie low, people said.

Greenbridge was a new pair of towers in Chapel Hill and John arrived like a migrating bird, to eat and sleep and disappear, people said. This was before Greenbridge went bankrupt, before John was in court, facing sex tapes and tell-all accounts.

But the buildings were mostly vacant at that time, empty at street level in the retail spaces that looked, when we walked by, like dark caves. And people said a friend of John's was the developer, who'd told John to use an apartment until the winds of disaster passed. A friend of ours who owned one of the market-price apartments in Greenbridge saw John in the elevator. And there were sightings, several of them, of John around the corner, at Bowbarr, drinking alone at five P.M.

Bowbarr is a tiny, dark bar on Rosemary Street that was designed to be low-at-heel, a long way from the bars at the Chapel Hill Country Club, or the Carolina Club, or the Siena Hotel, or wherever the town's favorite son used to drink, before the shunning.

But picture him there, in Bowbarr. A casual take: the same cut of hair, but no tie. Gin martini and small talk for the bartender, thumbing his tiny Blackberry wheel.

And the twentysomethings and thirtysomethings mashing alerts to their friends as fast as possible, *welp omg you guys john edwards @bowbarr ftw.*

Probably, he ran a tab. Probably, whenever John walked in,

the bartender put on Springsteen, because he knew John liked Springsteen. But *Nebraska*, not *Born to Run*.

I was an Edwards fan, once, and so was my wife. Now I just wish he'd go away. *John Edwards drinks at Bowbarr, he lives at Greenbridge*—for a while it was on so many lips.

2. Five years ago, we moved to North Carolina.

Five's my lucky number.

Basketball star Ty Lawson wore five, and so did Kendall Marshall, Ed Cota, Dexter Strickland, four of my favorite Tar Heels, though I always have to explain to people why Strickland made the list.

(Strickland was scrappy, he was fast, he had bad luck.)

I look out over a chunk of forest I still own in Chatham County. Our house just went into contract to be sold. We're moving to Los Angeles in February, to be fucked by Hollywood, consensually. My wife grew up in Chapel Hill, but she was born in Durham. Her grandfather on her dad's side worked in the tobacco market and sold firewood in Hayti. Her great-grandfather was a farmer. Her roots in North Carolina run deep; I have none.

The headline in this week's *Time* magazine: "John Edwards Returns to Personal-Injury Law, Personal Baggage and All."

It's November, five years since we arrived from France and bought a house. In the woods, there must be five hundred–plus shades of red and orange: tangerine leaves; Starburst leaves; leaves the color of bricks or dried blood.

I don't remember five years passing. Five years ago could be last night.

3. I did see John Edwards once at the Harris Teeter. He had admitted to the affair by that point, but not the child. We're two years out from court dates, sex tapes, the death of his wife. None of us know the future. He checks out at the same time as me, in another line. He looks skinnier. Heads turn. He's acutely aware of all of us. He avoids eye contact,

bags his own groceries, pays and leaves. Blue jeans, brown shoes, a simple T-shirt with a slogan on the chest.

4. Of course it's the T-shirt I'll remember the morning I die, when I've forgotten everything else, even my own mother's name: inscribed over a smiley face, "Life is Good."

5. I don't care about bbq.

6. Five years equals five autumns, five Halloweens, five times not a single child ate my candy.

For years I bought great candy bars: Kit-Kat, Snickers, Reese's Peanut Butter Cups. The first year I even bought full-size chocolate bars, not the minis. This year, I bought nothing.

This year, my wife's cousin Jamie joined us for a walk the day after Halloween. I complained about years of buying great candy for no audience, and he wondered, *Why do people always say they're better candy buyers than other people? What makes their candy so good?*

I said something like, *I buy candy I like to eat. It's about taste. No one wants to think their taste is bad. That's like admitting you're a bad driver, or you're bad in bed.*

But what if no one is a good candy buyer? What if you're either a buyer of candy or you're not, but there's no way to be good or bad at it, you just are or aren't, and this year I wasn't, the year we're leaving.

7. I do care about college basketball and it dates to the night my wife and I got engaged, thirteen years ago in a tiny motel outside Woodstock, N.Y., in the woods, near a lake, where there wasn't any cell phone reception, so we drove instead around the back roads with a bottle of cheap champagne until we found an old service station with a payphone where we could telephone our parents and tell them the good news, about our nuptials, and when my now fiancée put me on the phone, her mother was very lovely, telling me how excited

she was to welcome me into the family, then she said, to her husband, who was listening on the line, *Mike, do you have anything to say?* There's a pause so long I wondered if the line's been disconnected. Mike said, *Well . . . long pause . . . I'll just say . . . long pause . . . well, it takes a lot for a man to love his new son-in-law, when his new son-in-law doesn't know the first thing about Carolina basketball.*

8. I saw John Edwards at a Carolina game, once. Two minutes into it, he and two kids sat down across the aisle. They seemed to enjoy themselves. Everyone stood at the right times. Clapped for free throws. I didn't see John use his Blackberry once.

The guy sitting next to me said he'd seen John before at games, in the same seats. *Used to be he couldn't watch the game, so many people would stop and want to shake his hand.*

No one stopped by. No one shook his hand.

But maybe the guy made it up. Maybe he'd never seen John Edwards before in his life, except for on TV. Maybe he just needed something in that moment—a claim on the man who had disappointed so many.

What is John Edwards doing in this story?

8.a. From the *Time* article this week:

> Edwards, for one, believes that future juries will be able to see past his personal foibles. "I trust juries," he said in a recent interview with the *New York Times*. "They closely listen to the evidence that's presented to them. They listen to the law and, they collectively do what they believe is right. My years in courtrooms, both as a lawyer and in what I just went through, lead me to that same conclusion."

8.b. From *U and I*, by Nicholson Baker:

> Normally if I read something I think is wrong, I forget it two days later . . . but with Updike, when I disagree with

him, there is an element of pain, of emotional rupture, that makes me remember my difference, and as a result I keep returning unhappily to it over the years and checking to see whether the disaccord remains in effect—and because each time I check it I have to find grounds that will satisfy me for my continued refusal to be convinced by what he's said, I am able to refine my opinions in a way I could never do if I did find him universally agreeable.

9. One time, one of our neighbors asked if I'd kidnapped his dog. Another shot up a rental house with an AR-15. I normally get up at five A.M., and it's not uncommon in the late fall and early winter to hear hunters take shots in the dark.

Sometimes, when the weather was nice, one neighbor would drive up and down the road on his motorcycle wearing nothing but running shorts, flip-flops, and an American flag bandanna.

One neighbor wasn't so much a neighbor as a drug house, so we thought. Brick, bare, decrepit. We never saw anyone there. There was no appearance of occupancy, except the chimney was always smoking, blinds drawn. When there were cars in the driveway, they were always Porsches, Jaguars, Mercedes.

An angry neighbor once e-mailed the neighborhood listserv after encountering teenagers on the road wearing pants below their waists, exposing their underwear. He had not served in the Gulf to protect *that* freedom and had told them so, and wanted to tell us too. The angry neighbor was publicly reminded that the listserv was for coolheaded business, that was it.

10. Last year, down 15–501, toward Pittsboro, a waitress from the Carolina Brewery was found dead along Chicken Bridge Road, near Cruizer's. She was murdered, then set on fire. Some people driving by saw the fire and called 911. They tried, the newspaper said, to put out the fire with bottles of water while they waited for the police.

The killer recently got life in prison. A friend in the public defender's office told me he was evil, the kind of guy who prefers prison. I went to the courthouse for the trial's first day, to see him in person, but they shifted the date at the last second.

11. People never wanted to talk about the massage parlor on Franklin Street, next door to the left-wing bookstore. Plain front, no sign, just neon in the window that said GIRLS and the screen door in the back.

One guy who used their services told me he was too drunk at the time to complete the transaction, but would go again. Prices, he said, were actually pretty good. *It's not like it's a whorehouse or anything.*

Then something changed: the neon disappeared last year, replaced with a banner: *Under New Management / Tom Cats II.* (A little Googling will show you that Tom Cats is a Durham massage parlor, offering similar services.) Next, as of a month or two ago, even the banner was gone, replaced by a FOR RENT sign.

I went into the bookstore, asked what happened. The woman behind the counter said she had no idea. I asked if she knew what kind of business it had been. She said no.

12. Two weeks after we arrived, I tried renting a house off Craigslist. The owner replied and said he'd heard my name before and knew I was a writer, and he had a rule about not renting to writers. Turns out he was Duncan Murrell, contributing editor for *Harper's* magazine, and he was joking.

The next day I saw another house on Craigslist. I e-mailed the owner, he replied to say sorry, he'd just rented it to someone else. Then he wrote back an hour later to say he'd gone on to Google my name—he knew what it was like to have a weird name—and discovered I was a "fellow scribbler," maybe we could get a beer sometime. That was Wells Tower.

Daniel Wallace played basketball with my brother-in-law. Nic Brown needed a new tennis partner. Haven Kimmel was a friend of a friend and liked to drink martinis when the work was done. Instead of renting, we ended up buying a house and found that we now lived a mile down the road from Sam Stephenson, who invited us over for dinner, and Allan Gurganus arrived bearing flowers.

Bronwen, Jason, Matt, Andrew, Sean-y . . .

13. One time, Duke Libraries invited me to do an event, a reading plus lunch. For a parting gift, one of the librarians gave me a pink silk tie with blue devils embroidered into the fabric, each little devil holding a book. I wore the tie to Thanksgiving. In my wife's family, there isn't a single Duke fan. Her grandfather didn't even like people mentioning Duke at the table. We were into the wine when my father-in-law complimented the tie's bright color. I was sitting next to him. I told him to look more closely. *Oh my god*, he said, and looked sick.

14. We ate figs off our fig tree and blueberries from our bushes. My barber and I often fought about race relations. At Duke, at UNC, my students were generally terrific. I listened to Woody Durham, I listened to Jones Angel. Some nights we saw everybody, some nights we saw no one. Once, we were invited to participate in group sex. There were homes we went inside, as if by accident—*why did they invite us?*—that were so rich they had better paintings on the walls than museums, better wine in their wine cellars—they had real wine cellars—than any restaurant. We escaped in bars. We shot guns. The past became a trace, and the present was quickly tiring. I published two books, started two more. I drank my in-laws' wine. I met, through tennis, so many good-hearted men, and at Big Don's Garage, in Pittsboro, they even let me change my own oil. Family died, family was born. Seven days a week, we revised.

15. The *New York Post* reports John Edwards is dating a thirty-five-year-old single mom, a Duke employee. Recently they ate dinner at Panzanella in Carrboro, says the *National Enquirer*.

In *USA Today*, I read he's setting up a new law firm with his daughter in Raleigh, to tackle discrimination and consumer fraud cases. Meanwhile, also in Raleigh, Moral Mondays continue, the Republican rampage continues. So much is actually at stake. I was up at five A.M. today, it was dark outside, and a gun went off.

Goodbye, North Carolina. Like the T-shirt said, Life was Good.

Down East and the Coast

Chinquapin: Elementary Particles

RANDALL KENAN

1
THE THERE THERE

The Kenan Family Farm; Chinquapin; Duplin County; North Carolina; United States of America; Continent of North America; Western Hemisphere; the Earth; the Solar System; the Universe; the Mind of God.

34.8 degrees N latitude. −77.82 degrees W longitude. 39 feet above sea level.

The Northeast Cape Fear River. Creeks and brooks like lacework across the land, defining fields and forests. The northernmost edge of the Angola Swamp—home of Venus Flytraps.

Longleaf Pines and Oak and Sassafras. Maple, Sweetgum, Cedar. Laurel, Magnolia, Myrtle. Shortleaf Pine, Pitch Pine, Pond Pine, Eastern White Pine, Loblolly Pine. Sycamore. Cottonwood. Chokeberry. Hemlock. Elm. Pecan and Walnut trees. Orchards: Apple, Pear, Plum. Scuppernong Grape arbors. "Weeds" and wildflowers and grasses. Poke salad. (The American Chinquapin tree was practically wiped out by the Chestnut Blight between 1905 and 1940.)

Raccoon, opossum, squirrel, field mice. Insects. Frogs (tadpoles). Crayfish (Crawdaddies). Lamprey eels. Catfish. Bats. Rabbit. Deer. Bobcat. Muskrat. Black Bear. Alligators.

Chicken snakes, Rattlesnakes, King snakes, Black Racers, Coachwhips, Hog-nosed snakes, Green snakes, Garter snakes, Coral snakes, Milk snakes, Corn snakes. Cottonmouth moccasin.

Corn. Soybeans. Cotton. Cucumbers. Strawberries. Sweet potatoes. Peanuts.

Hogs. Cows. More hogs. Lots of hogs. Chickens. Turkeys. Even more hogs. Indeed, more hogs than people. Mules (already so few by now, in the 1970s).

Tobacco. Tobacco barns. Tobacco packhouses.

Tractors. Combines. Plows. Discs. Trucks. Truck beds.

The billboard: "You Just Missed It!"—1/2 mile back, Miss Sally's Diner.

Churches: First Missionary Baptist Church. St. Lewis Baptist Church. Sharon Baptist Church. Chinquapin Presbyterian Church. St. Mark Church of Christ. Mt. Horab Pentecostal Church. Church of Deliverance and Restoration Pentecostal Church. (Known affectionately as Holy Rollers.)

Cemeteries . . . and sparrows and thrushes and robins and cardinals and the occasional egret or heron. Quail/bobwhites. Hummingbirds, hawks, blue jays, mockingbirds. Woodpeckers. Turkey buzzards.

Stores: Speaker Thomas's Grocery Store. Billy Brinkley's Grocery Story. Parker & Sons' General Store and Supply. M. L. Smith & Sons (at Mills Swamp), known by everyone as "Luther Jim's."

The glorious ruins of a nineteenth-century train station: two stories, paint gone and dun and slowly falling down, the top balcony stubbornly holding on, defying gravity, the physics of collapse . . . burned down by the Chinquapin Volunteer Fire Department in 1981. The long abandoned rails of a train created to haul lumber at the turn of the nineteenth century. Rusty, overgrown, yet still there, even now . . .

Bank: United Carolina Bank. (Closed in 1987.)

United States Post Office.

Schools: Chinquapin Elementary #1 (formerly the black school); Chinquapin Elementary #2 (formerly the white school). Football. Basketball. Baseball. (Mascot: the Indians.). 4-H Club.

My mother's garden: snap beans (Kentucky Wonders), pole

beans, butterbeans, field peas, okra, cabbage, collards, mustard, Irish potatoes, carrots (sweet, sweet, sweet like candy; best straight from the earth—the dirt is good for you!), beefsteak tomatoes, cucumbers, onions, garlic, cayenne pepper, bell pepper, sweet corn, beets. Watermelon. (Begonias, wandering jew, dahlias, zinnias, geraniums, roses, sunflowers/black-eyed susans, snap dragons, azaleas . . .)

. . . There is more. Much, much more. Scents and tastes. The color of things. The sounds of laughter. The sound of dirt landing upon coffins. Hymns. Pop tunes on the radio. First loves. Vacation Bible School in June. Murders and talent shows. The time the carnival came to town . . . and for me *Star Trek* and Charles Dickens and Batman and *The Swiss Family Robinson* and Spiderman and *Treasure Island* and *The Hobbit* and the intense desire to be elsewhere. (How could I have forgotten blueberries?) And yet a funky good allegiance and gratitude. "Chickenpen, Nawf Cacalacky—smile when you say that, fella . . ."

Memory is a Polaroid.

"Location pertains to feeling; feeling profoundly pertains to place; place in history partakes of feeling, as feeling about history partakes of place," Eudora Welty writes in "Place in Fiction."

2

STRUCK BY LIGHTNING

Her: there was something about her that rubbed me the wrong way. Maybe it was the way she looked at me. Maybe it was the dip of snuff that never, ever, never left that place between her bottom lip and her gums; the way she spat the brown juice like a laser beam with enough accuracy and force to bisect a horsefly in midflight.

I got along with her sons, one was a grade ahead of me in school, one was a grade behind me. One was out of school.

One was a lap baby. Her daughter, Trisha, my age, never had a good word to say about me, and teased me without mercy. Her older daughter, Anne, looked upon me as if I had escaped from the pound, and wondered where the hell the dogcatcher was when you needed him most.

But with Miss Ella it was a matter of indifference, impatience, disregard. Maybe I wanted her to like me, and, once I sensed I was beyond any sort of such affection, I retaliated by disliking her more.

She was a large woman. Dark of skin. Lips large. Eyes deer-round and sad. She fancied sun dresses of the brightest hue. She complained often of the pains in her oversized feet, sandal-shod, toes painted fuchsia.

Their family was the poorest of the poor, which was mighty poor indeed in Duplin County. Tobacco season was the only time, truly, when they could augment government cheese and garden food with more store-bought food, when everyone could get day wages and the light bill would get paid. And everyone in the family worked. The baby was more often than not at the workplaces along with her. I don't remember much, if anything, about her husband. He never came to church. I wonder now if I ever laid eyes on him. Not that she ever came to church too often, except on those occasions when they served fried chicken, barbecue, slaw, potato salad, and iced tea afterwards. She never seemed to miss a funeral.

Nonetheless, when it came to tying tobacco, she was highly prized and sought after (also as a grader of cured tobacco). Her skills resided in her speed and in her accuracy. When she handed tobacco—a deceptively simple activity: three or four good-size leaves, the stems evened out with a pat of the heel of the palm, and backhanded to the tie-er—she accomplished the feat with Henry Ford–like automated precision, always the fastest hand in the South. When she tied—standing over a stick, suspended on a wooden and spindly "horse," grabbing the backhanded bunch of leaves, looping them in cotton twine, once, twice, and over, onto the stick, snug, one packet of bound leaves tight against the next, and the next, until the length of the wooden stick was full and tied off at the end: pop—she became a blur, a musician: zip, whir, zip, whir, zip, whir. God help you if you made her wait too long. And when the stick was complete, loaded down with big bunches of green leaves like oversized praying hands pointing downwards, she would grunt, "Stick!" This was my cue to come grab the done-thing and take it to a pile, which grew from nothing in the morning into a rectangular mountain of emerald by the end of the day. Her contempt for my slowness (or at least by her standards) was one of the burrs between us, when she would spit out the brown juice and say, "Come on, boy. Ain't got all day. You slow as Christmas coming. Where you at? Ham mercy."

I had been raised to respect my elders, to be courteous and gentle with all, to never sass back, and all that good Gospel Jazz. I did not enjoy the company of this woman.

That fateful day we were putting in tobacco for my cousin Seymour, who owned a small farm, but who also leased a great many acres from the bigger landowners. This certain field was remote from his farm, and the original barn there had long ago burned down. So we went about our toil on the edge of a copse of trees on the edge of this particular fifty acres of bright leaf. Under longleaf pines and oaks. A tarp had been strung over our heads to keep out the sun and the rain, but more important to give some protection to the stacked tobacco. It was a fairly flimsy setup, and the ground beneath our feet was uneven and rough and root-interrupted and grass-jagged and leaf-strewn. As much as I hated working in tobacco, not being under the proper shelter of a tobacco barn made this adventure even more hateful.

When the fields had been primed, we would load the pile of tied tobacco sticks onto a flatbed and haul it to one of Seymour's flue barns and hang it all there, high in the rafters, ready for firing—a hard day's work.

There was no Doppler Radar or Weather Channel in those

days. For all of us the day had begun before dawn, so not even Cousin Seymour had heard a weather report, not that anything short of a hurricane would have stopped the day's work. Cropping tobacco went on regardless of the temperature or precipitation. The show must go on.

The workday began bright and hot and blue skies. Sweat and dirt and black tar hands and tractor fumes and mosquitoes and snakes and plump, neon-green tobacco worms. Zip, whir, zip, whir, zip, whir. The workday was gossip about soap operas and whose husband was cheating on whose wife and who was in the hospital ailing with what and who had just lost his job and who was pregnant and who was moving back to North Carolina from New York. Zip, whir, zip, whir, zip, whir, zip, whir. The workday was aching backs and sore feet and dirt everywhichaway and sweat and bugs and dreams of sleep and supper and more cool water to drink.

I remember the clouds gathered with a breathtaking suddenness. All had been clear. Now the shadows grew and engulfed all. Dramatic enough to make all pause and take notice and comment: "Hmmm, child. Look like a storm is coming up." Day practically turned to night before the rain began. The wind already gusting. When the water droplets—fat aqueous pods to be more accurate—began to fall, at first vertical, and very soon horizontal, there was no time to retreat. Lightning crashed. Thunder truly rolled.

The makeshift tent failed promptly. We huddled, dark in the dark, torrents drenching, at the base of the largest, friendliest oak, wrapped up in the fallen, plastic blue tarp, the wind howling. I don't remember being afraid at all. Merely amused. After all that hot, it felt good to be wet, as if in a pool, all of a sudden. A number of us younger ones were giggling, snuggled up, after a fashion, in the dark and wet.

Lightning first, then thunder. You could hear the bolts striking in the distance. That's what creates the thunder. It is God's hammer slicing through the sky. The earth rocks. Graves shake. Hearts and time stop. The sound of over three million volts of electricity lancing down from the sky is a different sound. Thunder booms—the sound of electricity-cleaved air rushing back together. But lightning resounds more like an obliterating zap. Jove is angry. Ozone is in the air.

No wonder the old ones always made us young ones hush and be still every time a thunder cloud came up. They understood more about that terrible power than we could.

I don't remember the sound when it hit us, only that the insides of my eyes lit up. And the tell-tale tingle of electricity running through my being's fiber. Does sinew and muscle know it is being shot through with an abundance of electrons? What did Frankenstein's monster think when he was jolted back to life? How does the soul respond to electricity? Do androids ever dream of tobacco? I remember the pause before everyone hollered. Screamed. Shouted. I remember all of us hauling ourselves up, running ourselves to the trucks and cars. I remember fleeing in the rain and dark. I remember sitting in the car, everyone talking at once. "Jesus!" No one was dead. No one seriously harmed. The lightning had hit the oak; the energy flowing down into the earth, through us. We had been made, briefly, part of a circuit. I remember a soaked Miss Ella, sitting in the backseat of a Chevy Nova, moving her head, slowly, from side to side, and saying loudly, "Lord, Lord, Lord . . ." breathing heavily, as were we all.

"God was looking out for us," Cousin Seymour later said.

The next day I rode with him in his truck to see the sight. A great part of the oak tree was split, its whitish greenish-tan, vulnerable, wounded-looking innards exposed. Some sear on its bark. ("It resembled that perpendicular seam sometimes made in the straight, lofty trunk of a great tree, when the upper lightning tearingly darts down it, and without wrenching a single twig, peels and grooves out the bark from top to bottom, ere running off into the soil, leaving the tree still greenly alive, but branded."—Herman Melville, *Moby Dick*)

The next evening, after a long, long, long day of work, I remember returning home. I was bone-tired, recollecting powerful things for which I had no words, the feeling of electricity, the flash behind my retinas, the odd sense of camaraderie I shared with the fellow workers ("Did you feel that?"), thinking and wanting school to return in a few blessed weeks, when work would be done, and hot, dirty fields would be a hateful but necessary memory. I remember I was watching a Marty Feldman special on TV (*Marty Back Together Again*). I heard a car drive up and stop in the yard. I went to the door to see who it was. Miss Ella.

My mother greeted her on the front porch. Miss Ella said hey to me, pleasantly, but I stayed behind the screen door. I said Hey back. She had brought my mother tomatoes and collard greens. My mother oooed and aaahed her appreciation at the quality of the produce, and thanked Miss Ella and they sat in the white rocking chairs and talked. Only a few minutes, less than a full smoked cigarette in time. Just catching up. A wee touch of gossip.

"Well, I better get back," Miss Ella said, rising.

"Wait a minute," Mama said, and went to fetch some freshly picked okra for Miss Ella.

"Why thank you," she said. "Looks good."

For some odd reason I came out onto the porch to say, Bye.

She spat a hyper-fast snuff shot off the side of the porch, onto my mama's pansies. "That was something the other day, won't it?"

"Yes, ma'am," said I.

"Now you can tell folk you been struck by lightning." She let out an inky dark, earthy, loud, unrepentant witch's laugh. The very sound of it and the look on her face made me grin. She winked at me.

I watched as she got into her beat-up old Galaxy, a dull and unpolished metallic silver it was, and I watched it roll on down the dirt road, gaining speed as it went, dust rising up into the approaching-twilight air.

Those days of rattlesnakes and wild electrons were not lived, for me, like a character in a children's book, with warming hues and wonderful narrative arcs, and gentle old men walking me to the fishing hole imparting gentle wisdom about how to live a gentle life. More often than not there were mosquitoes and roadkill and spiteful gossip and raunchy tales I should have been spared. Neither were those days free of pettiness and bitterness and downright hatefulness and illness and rounding death. Those days were largely filled by a sense of lucklessness and a heavy dose of hard work, and seeing others work harder. In truth, Miss Ella treated me not much differently than she had before the lightning strike. Her life had not been altered much at all, but I knew mine would be. Such knowledge is at once a separation and a binding. What I did not know at the time was how indelible were those moments, those characters—people—that place, all of which would follow me all the way down my yellow-brick road.

Eudora Welty writes, in "Place in Fiction": "Where does the mystery lie? Is it in the fact that place has a more lasting identity than we have, and we unswervingly tend to attach ourselves to identity?"

A thing happened. A thing you shall never forget. It happened here, in a place that has known you and will always know you. By that knowing you are made.

Later that very summer, not the same day, but from the same porch, I would see the Aurora Borealis. Such a sight so very rarely seen so far south. Filling up the sky. Ghostly. Multicolored, yet largely, vastly green. Moving slow and yet not moving at all and lazy and with power beyond glory. Electrons spilling into our atmosphere. Above Cousin Norman's house, just across the road, above his barn, above the great oak tree that had lost its great twin in 1947, above the soybean field, above the forest and deer, above us all.

According to astronomical records that day was July 6, 1974. I was eleven years old.

Cutting Down Trees

BEN FOUNTAIN

Beyond the last of the barns and outbuildings on my grandparents' Martin County farm was a small patch of woods that's
still vivid in my mind. The land around it had been cleared
generations earlier for pasture and crops, but this little plot,
ten or twelve acres at most, formed a kind of forested trough
or vale, the land sloping to a shallow gully that ran down the
center. The grade was too steep, the bottom too marshy for
the place to be of much use, which is why it had been left to
woods, I suppose. There was a time in my late boyhood and
early adolescence when those woods had an unreasonable
hold on me. Or maybe not unreasonable; boys that age tend to
have the sensibility of a half-bright dog, so maybe it was per-
fectly normal that I would be up and out early in the morning
to scout those woods, walking the perimeter, tracking back
and forth across the middle, nosing around out of some animal attraction to the rich sensory textures of the place.

What was I doing out there? Walking and looking, walking
and looking—what was that about? With the slope, all the
crimps and folds of terrain, the early sun cutting through the
trees did amazing things. It seems to me now that I was trying
to comprehend something, trying to absorb all the shifting
variables of line, shape, color, and mass, all those spokes of
light and shadow cartwheeling through the trees. I must have
been trying to fix that patch of woods in my mind, out of an
instinct that it held something I needed to understand, and
that perhaps this sort of understanding wasn't a trivial thing.

One of my earliest memories is of a construction site: lot
scraped and graded, workmen moving about, the sound of

hammering, the sharp smell of freshly milled lumber. This was my family's house being built in Chapel Hill. I was around three years old, and my parents were making the leap to home ownership after the better part of a decade spent in graduate student dumps, one of which, as my mother used to recall with mortified wonder, *had snakes in the basement.*

Americans lived much closer to nature in those days. At some point during the construction my father's father, Ben Sr., came up from Rocky Mount to supervise the job. Granddaddy had spent most of his working life in law and politics, and still dressed every day in a dark suit and tie, but by then he was well into his second career as a small-town real estate mogul. He knew about building houses, so here he was in Chapel Hill to build ours. Loud, short, stout, with a headful of silky white hair and rimless eyeglasses, he looked so much like Mr. Dithers of the "Dagwood" comic strip that for several of my preliterate years I just assumed that was my grandfather who showed up in the funnies every couple of days.

He was manic-depressive, though of course I didn't know it at the time. To me he was simply a lively and somewhat agitating presence, a nice man with a jackhammer voice who chain-smoked Kent cigarettes and dominated conversation. Later in life I'd learn how his bouts of spectacular activity would be followed by the inevitable crash, but when he was up, Granddaddy was a hard man to manage. Maybe his visit coincided with a manic phase; that seems to leak into my adult understanding of the story, a whiff of berserk energy that led to the razing of all the dogwood trees. Those trees were chief among the reasons my mother had chosen this lot, the way the front yard's graceful slope was gently punctuated by a string of seven or eight mature dogwoods. With their delicate pastel blossoms in spring, their berries and russet foliage in fall, and even a sentimental Christian legend inspired by its flower, the dogwood is one of the sacred trees of the South. Nobody cuts down a dogwood unless they have to—nobody but a madman?

It's one of our family's totemic stories, Granddaddy cutting down all of Mom's dogwood trees. She stopped by the house one morning and everything was fine; when she returned that afternoon the trees were gone. I must have been with her when she drove up to the house and saw the lot scraped clean, and it's probably worth an experiment in hypnosis to try to recover my toddler's memory of what she said. If she blew up, that part of the story has been suppressed, though given the ways of our family I doubt there was any blowup. Silence, seething resentment, the lifelong burn, these are more our style. The air of cynicism that flavors the story probably came later, an effect of my parents' long and difficult marriage. When I was old enough to ask what she'd done that day, my mother's reply was curt, soft-pedaled with a laugh.

"Nothing I *could* do. Those trees were gone."

Granddaddy had a saying: "A vacant lot's not good for anything but holding the world together." Whatever its shortcomings, this point of view can't be said to lack focus, a bracingly stripped-down approach that consigns much of the earth to standby status while requiring every place and thing to have its use. Granddaddy seems to have been a fair representative of my paternal line, an obsessive-compulsive Scotch-Irish clan characterized by thrift, caution, and tight control over self and others, along with an unspoken but enduring assumption that in the getting and keeping of money, one's anxieties might be eased. They were not mellow people, the Fountains; hard work and worry were wired deep in the DNA.

"We're middle-class, I suppose," Dad said one night at the dinner table. I would have been fourteen or fifteen by then, old enough not only to follow his meaning but to sense the disconnect. "Middle-class at best," he amended. "Probably lower middle-class. Not much chance of moving up. A lot more chance of moving down."

These words were spoken in the kitchen of our five-bedroom, three-bath Colonial on the golf course of MacGregor

Downs Country Club in Cary, N.C. Mom had succeeded in keeping this lot—almost an acre—fully wooded; Granddaddy had been dead for several years by then. For summer vacation, instead of playing golf or taking his family on trips like other men, Dad would spend that time cutting down supposedly dead trees in our little patch of woods. Of course he made me help him, and these were awkward, mostly unpleasant days. We weren't used to doing things together, and he was bossy, and I was in my stubborn midteens, and resented the fact that we were out there chopping down trees just because he couldn't think of anything better to do on his vacation. We argued. Dead trees eventually fall down on their own, I pointed out, and often what he culled looked very much alive to me. The sickly, the stunted, the merely funny-looking, his default inclination was to cut them all, and pretty quickly it became apparent to me that I'd been drafted into a covert logging operation. Like his father before him, Dad had no use for trees, and not to footprint the entire lot made him deeply unhappy. The peace of his marriage depended on letting those woods be, but to leave it at that was just too much for his nervous system. He needed to cut, so he would cut as much as he could, mindful that Mom was keeping an eye on us from the house.

It's obvious to me now that he took no pleasure in the job. Outdoor activity was never his thing, and the work was slow, hot, tedious, and clumsily done on both our parts—neither one of us was even remotely handy. Because he distrusted chainsaws, our tools were a rust-barnacled ax and a bow saw from Sears. We fought, often, bitterly, with real malice. He showed no instinctive feeling for trees, whereas I viewed them with a dreamy kid's bent for romance. Tolkien was a powerful influence on me in those days, along with lingering vapors of flower power left over from the sixties. I was open to the possibility of some mystery or meaning in nature that had no traction in Dad's universe.

"We ought to just clear the damn place," he'd huff several times a day, usually when the work had bogged down and he was fed up with it all. His preference, often expressed, was for a lush green lawn and circular driveway, a suburban image of order and ease that seemed, like a mirage on the near horizon, to hold out the promise of a worry-free life.

I once asked Dad if the Depression had hit his father hard.

"*Very* hard," he answered gravely, in tones other people might use to recall a death in the family. "He lost several of his farms outside Rocky Mount."

This gave me another disconnect to mull over: if you'd had several farms to lose, then maybe you hadn't done so badly. My mother's family had that one farm in Martin County, on which they lived and made their living, and while they surely existed much closer to disaster than my father's family, they seemed to suffer less anguish from the prospect. My maternal grandfather, Julian, was what social historians call a "yeoman farmer," the agrarian version of middle-class. Half of the farm was in pasture and cultivation, while the other half consisted of hardwood forest that backed up to a bend in the Roanoke River. These woods were very old second growth, an echo of the vast oak forest that once covered the entire eastern seaboard. Dense, humid, funky, in summers greener than Vietnam, the woods held beech, poplar, maple, sweet gum, at least a dozen subspecies of oak, and where the land fell off to swamp, cottonwood, and cypress. As a young man, Julian had seen bald eagles and flying squirrels in these woods, and while such wonders were long gone, it was still a wild place. Deer, fox, bobcat, and turkey were common, as were opossum, raccoon, game birds, and packs of feral dogs. Some years there were signs of bear; rumors of panther cropped up from time to time, and the area was a semitropical stew of snakes.

My family lived in towns—Chapel Hill, Elizabeth City, Kinston, Cary—but holidays and much of the summers I spent on my grandparents' farm. That's the place, more than anywhere, that formed me, and where for most of my childhood and adolescence I wanted to be, following Julian around as he did the daily work of the farm, or tagging along with my male cousins—both older, both born and raised on my uncle's farm down the road—on chores and hunting trips. For a while they had a motorcycle, which we rode bareheaded and free all over those dirt roads. On hunting trips I carried a gun but never managed to shoot anything, and that was fine; like the dogs, I was ecstatic just to be tramping around the woods. Years later, reading the Saul Bellow novel *Humboldt's Gift*, I encountered Von Humboldt Fleisher's interpretation of Wordsworth's career, which was essentially that of a poet who'd had a series of intense mystical experiences in nature during his youth, and spent the rest of his life trying to make sense of them through poetry. Is that what had happened to me? Maybe, though on a much less rarified level. My adolescence coincided with the heyday of Tolkien and the *Foxfire* books, and heavy reading of those fueled my already hyper infatuation with the natural world. Then came Hemingway, who nearly undid me. We were assigned "Big Two-Hearted River" in sophomore English; I remember sitting down to read it one night at the kitchen table in Cary, and feeling dazed, knocked loose from myself by the end. It was a story in which nothing seemed to happen, and yet everything seemed to happen, and that "everything" was bound up in Hemingway's careful rendering of the natural world. I wanted more, and set out to read everything by him that I could get my hands on. At some point it must have occurred to me that the pleasure one got from reading stories of this sort would be hugely magnified by writing one's own, assuming you could make them halfway good. At any rate, it was around this time that I began to try to write. I have vague memories of producing what must have been some epically bad Hemingway imitations, but thankfully all those pages disappeared a long time ago.

For one hunt, my cousins and I put on the highest boots we could find and tramped directly into the swamp, following the hummocks and low ridges that formed a kind of soggy archipelago through the standing water. Eventually we passed from family property onto Weyerhaeuser land, which could have been ours, my cousins said. All this, hundreds, maybe thousands of acres, and they proceeded to tell me a story about our great-grandfather, how in the 1890s he supposedly trekked back here with an eye to acquiring the property. It was his for the taking; he only had to assume the taxes, but the area was so remote, so swampy, so miserable with snakes and bugs, that neither he nor anyone else wanted anything to do with it. Now the timber was worth a fortune! And so our family had missed its chance at fabulous wealth.

You heard it all the time in eastern North Carolina, that so-and-so had "sold timber." These sales made people rich, after a fashion, for a while; a new house might appear, new cars, maybe some redneck extravagance like a motor home or a speedboat. But drive any distance down the highway and you'd see the other side of the equation, the tracts of recently timbered land that looked as blasted as those photos of Verdun or the Somme from World War I. There was something dire, vaguely shameful, about selling timber. I never heard anyone say as much outright, but a kind of solemnity attached to any conversation on the subject, the diffidence of people broaching some species of taboo. The rural Carolina culture that was degraded in so many ways—racist, insular, grasping, shrill in its pride of tobacco and rotten with guilt—could muster enough integrity for this at least, a collective awareness that selling timber was business of a different degree. There was something irredeemable in it, on a scale that evoked biblical overtones. Often the land had been in the family for generations, and so to log it, to cash out on that long-standing capital, could seem as drastic as selling your birthright for a bowl of mush. That gutted landscape was what you and your heirs had to look at from the windows of your new house, your fancy new car. The cost was right there in your face, not numbers on paper, not concepts in some abstract moral calculus, and the consequences were stark enough to make most people hesitate.

If you owned timber, the temptation was always there, but timber money had a funny way of disappearing. It was all very public, the way the sellers would spend rich for a couple of years, then gradually slide back to their original level. Even so, many sold; it was just too much money to resist. For others, my grandfather Julian among them, the issue was never up for discussion. Then there was my uncle's family, which included those two cousins I'd spent half my life following around. Hosea—he was named after the Old Testament prophet—was my mother's only sibling. He was a teenaged tail gunner in World War II, and upon making it home from the war in one piece he was given half the farm by his father, Julian. In his early forties Hosea worked and smoked and stressed himself into a near-fatal stroke that left him permanently disabled, and from that point forward the family spiraled deep into debt. Selling timber seemed one way to save the situation, for the short term at least. My aunt was for it, and her and Hosea's oldest daughter; my two male cousins, not so much. In the end it came down to Uncle Hosea. Damaged as he was, crippled, reduced by half, he still had his legal capacity, and summoning the mysterious, maddening stubbornness that the infirm are sometimes capable of, he dug in his heels and refused to sell.

The struggle went on for years, a long-running soap opera with complex maneuverings, factions, rumors, and moments of high drama, all the dysfunctional functioning and emotional turmoil of a family in the throes of a financial crisis. For a while we kids went through a Ouija Board phase, and one night my cousin Pam asked the board, "Will Daddy *ever* consent to selling timber?," with Hosea himself sitting there not six feet away. It was just the air we breathed, this drumbeat of money aggression. Now, forty years later, I wonder why he wouldn't sell, and it strikes me as strange that I never heard him say. Same for Julian—I don't remember reasons ever being given. In that time and place, two or three hundred thousand dollars seemed like all the money in the world. So much wealth, so easily had; something powerful must have been at work to counterbalance that, something as real to those two men as anything in their lives. I don't remember them as being at all sentimental or precious. They weren't conservationists, not in the latter-day sense of the fate of the planet hanging in the balance. They seemed to care little about aesthetics, natural or otherwise. Yet what must have been at work—*had* to have been at work—was a profound conviction in the value of those woods as an entity in itself. Some vital, intrinsic worth inhered in its existence, something genuine and real that surpassed the prospect of a small fortune. Nothing else explains it. The place was worth preserving, even worth forgoing more money than any of us could imagine, and for them the fact was so self-evident that they never felt the need to explain themselves.

Hosea never sold. In his sweet, dogged way he stood his ground and resisted all forms of appeal and harassment. Time passed, and eventually people started dying. Julian went in 1976, Hosea in 1981, my maternal grandmother in 1983. My mother inherited her parents' farm, which my cousins fiercely resented; that Julian had given their father half of the original farm was ancient history and conveniently forgotten. Relations were tense, but civil; for another year or two we all gathered at Christmas. With Hosea's passing, it was assumed that my aunt and cousins would soon sell their timber, but they hesitated, put off selling to the indefinite future, and it strikes me as the neatest of ironies that now the issue jumped to our side of the family, Dad pushing Mom to sell off all the timber she inherited. "That farm's not worth anything," he'd been saying for years, maligning the prospects for her inheritance—his way of preemptively putting her on the defensive, I suppose. It wasn't that they needed the money—they were secure, more than comfortable. This was just Dad being Dad, his nervous system demanding that tangible profit be wrung from the place. My sisters and I begged them not to sell, but this was the nostalgia argument, and not so compelling for Mom, who had to live with the real-time burden of it. There was the worry and hassle of upkeep, my cousins' passive-aggressive sniping, and the grief that came of having to think about the place, the reminder that her parents and brother were gone. Even before the beatdown of Dad's timber campaign, Mom was worn out with the place. Maybe she hoped that selling timber would earn her some breathing room.

By degrees the deal was rationalized. Simply to leave the woods as is was "not good land management." Once the timber was cleared, Weyerhaeuser would replant the land with fast-growing pine seedlings, which would lead in time to future "harvests." And not everything would be cut—the stands of trees near the home place would be spared. And so on, until Mom finally agreed.

I couldn't stand to think about it, so I didn't, a nonresponse made easier by the fact that I was living in Texas by then. So the timber was sold, the woods duly obliterated, the proceeds added to Dad's strategically laddered portfolio of time deposits, and within the year Hosea's three oldest children sued my parents. How could they not? That's the thought one has in retrospect. The ruination of the land they'd grown up on, which they felt by rights was theirs, and to which they surely had some very real psychic ownership—to see it wrecked right under their noses demanded a response. My cousins couldn't sue Mom for selling her own timber, of course, so they ginned up some bogus allegations asserting fraud and malfeasance in her handling of her parents' estate, a primal scream of a lawsuit that bounced around the courts for a couple of years and was eventually dismissed.

Jesus would weep at the whole sorry mess of it. After netting out taxes, the cost of replanting, and attorneys' fees, how much did my parents actually clear from the timber? I asked Dad not long after the lawsuit was dismissed. He shrugged,

Cutting Down Trees

175

pretended disgust. He was as aware as anyone of what a shit show the whole thing had been. In his view it simply furnished more proof, as if any was needed, of how hard it is to get ahead in life. I waited for his answer, knowing to allow a wide margin for his tendency to poor-mouth.

"Twenty-five thousand," he snorted. "Maybe thirty."

Such a piddling amount of money, when it was all said and done. Family ruptured. Land ravaged. Our life in that place was over.

What was I doing out there all those years ago, those mornings I spent tramping around the woods behind the barns? In retrospect, it seems neither more nor less momentous than that I was stumbling toward awareness of my own human senses. This awareness—is it a version of grace, I wonder, or a rough working version, the raw stuff in all its necessary potential. A few years after the timber sale, I asked my mother about that patch of woods. Had it been cut, or was it close enough to the house that they'd left it alone? She was uncertain, so I described the place for her, that shallow gully with the huge oak trees along the bottom. She still didn't know what I was talking about. She could only say what she'd always said, that some stands of trees near the house had been left intact.

Eventually she sold the house and a couple of acres around it, to a man who promised to, and did, restore the house to what it had been before a decade of vacancy had reduced it to near ruins. I haven't been back in thirty years, since my grandmother died. For a long time I assumed I would, but at some point I began to resist the notion, out of a sense that in seeing it again, something might be lost. I don't have the guts to go back, put it that way. Whatever is good and decent in me owes something to the place, and to those woods that I still return to in my mind. To see them gone would, it seems, diminish me in some way. Or maybe it would just hurt too much, and to no purpose. Better to leave it as is, in my mind, at least. Whatever it was I found out there, I need it still.

Writing from the Rim

JAN DEBLIEU

On a pretty, breeze-cooled summer afternoon, I stashed some drinks and a towel in a daypack and met up with some friends on the bank of a brand new river. Hesitating for a few moments—was this really safe?—we jumped in and rode the insistent current down to the sea.

Warm green water and skittling foam: we floated along belly-up, laughing and splashing, our arms and legs splayed out. Eddies spun our bodies around. Just as we reached the Atlantic, our bottoms bumped against a sandbar. We climbed out, water streaming from us, and trotted upstream to do it again.

It was a blast. It was as novel as the briny river itself, cut through Hatteras Island by a hurricane the previous year. As we clambered from the inlet a second time, I wanted to be exactly where I was, on the rim of a continent where rivers come and go and nothing is certain except change.

My home is on the North Carolina Outer Banks. I've dug in and convinced my husband, Jeff, that we must live here, only *here*, because of the islands' ability to constantly surprise me. It is a quality that provides moments of stomach-churning dread, usually at the height of storms, as well as a deep contentment and plenty of fun. I've never known anywhere like this, a land where the geology can be swept clean overnight. Living here has made me wake up to my life. In the process it has helped me learn how to write.

My love affair with the Outer Banks had the most inauspicious of beginnings.

It was 1984. Jeff and I had made plans to drive up from Atlanta and meet an old friend for a May vacation in Rodanthe, a Hatteras Island village that back then really looked like a village. As we drove into town, we couldn't get over the scoured sparseness of the land. A single dune stood by the ocean. Behind it, the sand was spottily covered with brown grasses and prickly brush. Among the squat, weathered houses, a few salt-scorched pines stood in sorry groves.

We turned our attention to the ocean, which was indeed lovely, if a little rough and cold. After being trounced several times by the merciless breakers, we opted to stay on the deck of our trailer-like cottage-on-stilts and work on our tans. We planned lavish meals that went uncooked for lack of ingredients. There were no decent grocery stores for miles. One morning we woke at 7:00 to the rumbling of a backhoe just beyond the bedroom wall. As we spilled bleary-eyed onto the porch, the owner of the cottage next door called, "We're just going to move a little sand." The racket continued for three days. Still, we managed to have fun, taking dozens of pictures of ourselves holding fruity drinks in the splendid spring light. They ended up looking like ads for some kind of rum.

We drove off the island at the end of the week, not sorry to be going home. Who could have predicted that the following spring I'd be back for good with a book contract?

Up to that point I'd written plenty of newspaper and magazine articles, but nothing of length. I'd taken one college course on seaside ecology, the supposed subject of my "creative island narrative." My publishing contract was with a company that had yet to put out its first volume. Undaunted, I convinced Jeff to move from a trendy section of Atlanta into a dilapidated if historic island house that had most recently played host to a half dozen surfers. After we applied several coats of paint and convinced the landlord to put in new carpet, the interior was passably clean and free of bugs.

Gradually we began to meet the locals. They had watched us from afar, impressed by our efforts to turn the local drug den into a home suitable for a couple with something like family values. Their initial approval waned after they learned that while we claimed to be married, we didn't share a last name.

We found that Rodanthe had plenty of characters, and some would chat a little if we said hello. Among them were four stout and stalwart Hatteras women, all of whom lived close by.

Marilyn and Mildred were sisters-in-law. Marilyn and her husband, a good-hearted if impetuous man, owned a gas station and convenience store two doors down from our house. Most mornings I went to the store to buy a newspaper. Mildred always greeted me with a slow, sweet smile and a "How are you?" She had a pale, doughy face that seemed like it had never seen the sun—surprising in a beach town. But she didn't like wind, cold, heat, bugs, or anything else that came with being outdoors on Hatteras. Over time I came to know her as someone who wished nothing but good for others. Marilyn, the blond of the duo, was gruff at first but warmed up to us as we stayed on. Who could blame her? She'd seen countless city types move to town. Usually they didn't last, not on a sandy reef so far out to sea that the electricity tended to give out in high winds. This happened several times a week. No one had generators, not back then. Instead we had hurricane lamps and gas ranges and spare bottles of water.

Virginia—Ginny to her friends—was the local postmistress. We'd visit for a few minutes whenever I went to check our post office box. She helped me construct an understanding of who lived where in the village and how they were related. Ginny was a widow; her husband had drowned in Pamlico Sound one day while out checking his fishnets. His empty boat had run aground in a marsh. For months, Ginny had searched the island's banks with the hope of finding his body. One morning in church she had a vision of the spot where she would find him, on a little knoll in a nearby marsh. After the service she went to the place with her cousin. Her husband's body was there, face down. Village residents swore to the truth of this story. I wrote it down and put it in my book.

The fourth woman who colored my early months on Hatteras was Zenovah, a forbidding matron from Fair Haven United Methodist Church. Zenovah didn't like me.

I noticed her the first time we attended one of the wonderful, if starchy, weekly Chicamacomico chicken dinners. These were held in the local community center, which bore the original Indian name for the village. Local women dished up big servings of stewed chicken, dumplings, white rolls, baked beans, and canned green beans. Marilyn was there, businesslike as she handled the till but smiling hello, and Ginny, bustling to get us food like we were her favorite grandchildren, and a stern, heavyset woman with strawberry hair that stood up from her forehead in a shellacked wave. She wore oversize glasses that were straight from the 1970s. It was no longer the 1970s. She took one look at us, tightened her mouth, and handed me the smallest roll on the tray.

Was I imagining her snub? When I asked Jeff, he said he hadn't noticed anything. I shook off my misgivings, dug into the food, and went back to worrying about how to write a creative island narrative.

When I wasn't waiting tables, I spent my hours walking the beach or poking around the marsh with binoculars, a magnifying loop, and a few plastic bags in which I could bring home interesting finds. I passed the evenings writing in my journal or bent over a field guide at our kitchen table, which had been built from old Coast Guard crates. I reminded myself of a crusty Victorian gentleman.

One afternoon in the shallows of Pamlico Sound, a brilliant green seaweed caught my attention. I waded out, plucked a few leaves, and stuck them in my pocket. Back home, I stuffed them into a glass canister filled with water. They fanned out prettily, allowing me to identify them as sea lettuce. To my surprise, tiny specks swarmed from them. My field guide informed me that they were a species of arthropod commonly known as scuds. They lived in the canister, munching on the sea lettuce and enthusiastically reproducing, for several months. Dinner guests were not impressed.

Late one night, driving the sleepy miles home from the restaurant in Nags Head where I worked, I was jolted awake by three strange white chips on the road. They had deeply bowed legs, and they ran toward the car brandishing huge claws — huge, that is, considering that the critters themselves were only three inches tall. Ghost crabs. A few mornings later I happened to be walking on a secluded beach when I noticed pairs of these land-meets-sea marvels locked in ferocious shoving matches. They ran toward each other, brandishing their pearly claws, and collided roughly, pushing each other forward and back in a contest for — what? The prettiest female? The choicest location for a hole in the sand? Scientists, I learned, had no idea.

Roaming through the Pea Island National Wildlife Refuge, I found the hidden haunts of night herons and the oversize stacks of twigs used as nests by black-neck stilts, the most elegant birds I'd ever seen. I talked to fishermen about their adventures and to marine scientists about their studies. I wrote it all down.

I did not write much about the messier side of island living: the sulfurous well water that stained our clothes, the exorbitant price of groceries and gas, and the host of biting bugs — chiggers, greenhead flies, yellow deer flies, and mosquitos. I'd smack these bloodsuckers with all my might, only to watch them fly off unharmed. One morning at breakfast, a tick fell out of my hair and into my cereal. I flicked it out of the milk and kept eating.

Nor did I chronicle our personal complications. After two months of hard labor packing fish and running a string of crab pots, Jeff was offered a great job back in Atlanta. How could he refuse? Our life on Hatteras was draining our bank account. We agreed to try a temporary, long-distance marriage, while our friends and family worried that we were splitting up. I assured them we were not. We couldn't; I needed him too much. Besides being my love, he was the best editor with whom I'd ever worked.

Alone and lonely, I sank myself into the book, feeling my way along, sharply conscious that I had never written anything longer than sixteen double-spaced pages. I divided my potential subjects into chapters and started trying to write about them as I always had written, as a newspaper and magazine journalist. Just the facts, ma'am.

I found I couldn't do it. It was too shallow an approach. As the months passed, I realized I felt more alive on Hatteras than anywhere I'd ever lived. I was no longer a mere observer; I had to write about what it was like to celebrate waking up every day on Hatteras. And so I committed the cardinal sin: I pushed aside the boundary of objectivity. I became someone who wrote about her feelings and deep love of a place.

Who wouldn't be fascinated by this landscape, or seascape (both terms were apt), with all its subtleties? When I'd moved to Hatteras, I had looked forward to living in a natural system that was almost entirely untouched by humans. I was quickly disabused of that notion. The towering, grassy dunes I so loved were artificial. They had been built in the 1930s and '50s by government workers, in an attempt to protect houses and roads from the fury of the ocean. Not only had this failed, it was causing the island to wash away. Who could have foreseen such a thing? A slice of windswept ground that baffled scientists: who wouldn't want to stay here forever?

Socially, things weren't so great. I made a few friends, most of whom lived miles away, too far for frequent get-togethers. In Rodanthe my status had shifted from respectable to pitiful. One day a fisherman dropped off some of his catch for me, a gesture of charity for the abandoned woman whose not-husband had run off to Atlanta.

Ginny, Marilyn, and Mildred continued to be comfortably

kind to me, and Zenovah barely civil. As the months wore on, it became clear that I would have to leave Hatteras and join Jeff in Atlanta. We simply couldn't afford two households. Also, our Hatteras house wasn't heated or insulated. Were I to stay, I could look forward to a winter of solitary, shivering nights.

I surrendered and helped Jeff load the furniture into another U-Haul for the trip back. In the city again, I set up my office on the sun porch of the charming two-bedroom house Jeff had rented. I got back in touch with our old friends and tried to be happy. It didn't help that my writing required me to immerse myself in memories of Hatteras. Later, Jeff would tell me that during this period I reminded him of a beautiful tropical bird confined to a cage. There was nothing to be done about it. For the sake of love, I had clipped my own wings.

Some people say there is no such thing as coincidence. At times I wonder. All I can tell you is that during my first nine months on the Outer Banks, I came to feel as if I belonged there. And six months after my departure, the stars aligned to bring us back. Jeff's job in Atlanta turned out to be much different and less satisfying than he'd been led to believe. But while there, he made a friend who had another friend who needed a man like Jeff to fill a position on the coast. By the following April we were able to come back.

This time the firm that hired Jeff paid for our move. When the Mayflower van pulled up to our same little house in Rodanthe (I hoped the neighbors were watching!), we went inside to find that the carpet still held indentations from where our tables and couch had sat the previous year. We'd been gone no time at all.

There was just one complication. I had disconnected our telephone, and the phone company had quickly reassigned the number. No real problem; I arranged for another. But the original number remained under Jeff's name in the phone book.

One afternoon I ran into Zenovah at a local store. She gave me a look that shocked me with its disdain. What had I ever done to this woman?

After I paid for my purchases, I went out to the parking lot to find Zenovah waiting for me. "I know what you're up to," she said in a caustic tone.

I tried to smile. "What?"

"I know what you do when your husband's at work. Don't try to tell me otherwise." She looked me up and down, her eyes narrowed and full of contempt. "I called your number last week. I wanted to ask you to make something for the bake sale." She moved closer as if spoiling for a fight. "A man answered," she nearly spat, "and it was the middle of the day." She nodded once and spun on her heel.

I stood doltishly on the pavement as she stalked away. My number? "Wait," I called, "That's not our number anymore!" But she was already in her car with the windows up.

I'd heard from other transplants about the cliquishness of Hatteras natives, and how they'd shut out newcomers for no reason. Zenovah wasn't a bad woman; she thought she was defending her village from a serious moral threat. But it stung me to be so summarily tried and condemned.

For a few days I was cautious in my dealings with locals. I watched closely for any hint of judgment but found none. Ginny, Mildred, and Marilyn were as friendly as ever. No one but Zenovah seemed to care about my perceived harlotry. Gradually I relaxed. Nonetheless, I had a new appreciation for what I'd heard laughingly called Hatteras's Wild West mentality. Besides a love for hard drinking and fighting, it had a third ingredient Jeff described as mean-spiritedness. I could see it in the way some men and women carried themselves. Don't cross me, it telegraphed, or you will be made to suffer.

It is easy to fall in love with the beauty of a place, harder to accept and ultimately forgive its flaws. Too often these appear in the form of bigotry and hatred. Every writer must learn to find the humanity within such behavior. I had settled in a place that would give me ample opportunity to hone that skill.

When my book finally came out, the publishing company gave me 100 copies to be distributed to Hatteras locals. I dropped them off to the people I knew and waited.

A man named Bruce, whom I'd barely met, was incensed. "If you really cared about us," he snarled, "you'd of made sure every local got a copy of your damn book."

"Don't pay no attention to him," Bruce's cousin told me. "He's drunk."

A month later, Bruce approached me at the post office. He tapped me on the arm as I was leaving.

I looked at him hesitantly, expecting another barrage.

"Want to tell you," he said, "that book of yours? You got it right."

I felt as if I were flying as I skipped down the post office steps.

Jeff and I were islanders now. But by the time we had amassed the money to buy a house, the Hatteras real estate market had climbed beyond our reach. We found a place we loved on Roanoke Island and sadly left Rodanthe. We consoled ourselves with the knowledge that we were lucky to have found a way to stay on the Outer Banks. I moved on to other writing projects and visited Hatteras as often as I could. Jeff resigned as my editor. We agreed it was healthier for our marriage.

For my third book I decided to write about the wind, which defines the islands as much as it shapes the surrounding waters. Much of my research involved collecting stories from people who had survived storms.

One afternoon, my friend Jim took me to a house on Hatteras where a fisherman he knew was adding a sun porch to the second floor. The owner, whom I'll call George, had once gotten caught in a strong squall offshore. The boat on which he was fishing had barely made it back to shore.

George was more than happy to knock off work for a few minutes to relate the tale. He cracked open a beer as we sat down with him on the unrailed decking. Our legs dangled over the edge. I tried not to look at the ground, fifteen feet below.

At the height of the storm, George told us, the captain stood "out on the foredeck, waving his fist and hollering. Wicked winds, and the waves higher than a two-story house." George was a handsome man, and he knew how to spin a yarn. "When the cap came back to the wheelhouse, I asked him what he'd said out there. 'I told the Lord, Goddamn it, you've sunk boats out from under me twice before, but you can't have this one. You're not going to beat me this time.'" George shook his head and said, "I didn't fish with him after that."

A large Chevy sedan, its maroon paint dulled by salt air, pulled into the driveway. George straightened up. "Uh-oh," he said. "Here I am, jawin' with you, and I'm supposed to be working. I'll catch it now."

A familiar figure heaved her body from the driver's seat and gave her strawberry hair a protective pat. I knew that hair-style and body shape, and those oversized glasses. Zenovah. A pretty brunette slid from the passenger side. "That's my wife," George said from the side of his mouth, "and mother-in-law."

I became acutely aware of where we were sitting. The second-floor porch, which opened off the master bedroom.

Jim gave a big grin. "Time to go," he said.

A year and a half later, George was drawn into a feud with another Hatteras fishermen. The circumstances are murky, but one day George ended up beneath the wheels of his rival's car. His injuries proved fatal.

Two years after Hurricane Irene, I stood with my elderly parents on the bank of the inlet cut by the storm, the same sluice where my friends and I had played. When we moved to Hatteras, Mom and Dad had still been in their middle years. Now it was Jeff and I whose hair was turning gray. I led my parents carefully to the edge of the inlet. Water no longer washed completely through; the channel was in the process of closing. Cars and trucks banged across a metal bridge that looked as if it had been soldered together from pieces of an old Erector Set. Locals called it the temporary permanent bridge.

I pointed to a spot half a mile offshore where the color of the ocean changed from green to a murky blue. "See that line out there?" I asked Mom and Dad.

They did.

"When I moved here, the road was all the way out there." The ocean had since claimed it, and all the land in between.

My mother shook her head. "I'm glad you live on these islands and not me."

I smiled. "Me too," I said.

Change is constant, and also necessary for growth. By that measure, life on the Outer Banks has offered me more than enough nourishment for learning what it means to write. The islands' people have befriended me, loved me, challenged me, disparaged me, puzzled me, and at times brought me to tears. They have taught me about humanity and humility. The wisest have shown me the folly of opposing nature, which will most certainly win any contest or fight. On my journey along the road of stories, I have traveled to many exotic places. But I have never been sorry to come home.

A Man Came Up from Wilmington, Carrying a Bag of Snakes

MICHAEL PARKER

When people in other parts of the country ask me why so many writers come from North Carolina I am always tempted to tell them that, proportionally, there are just as many people with messed up psyches in North Carolina as there are in New Hampshire, County Cork, or Calcutta. So it stands to reason that a fraction of these walking wounded would try to repair the rents in their psyches by writing novels and stories and poems about people trying to repair the rents in their psyches. Just like in New Hampshire, County Cork, Calcutta.

Yet the notion that we turn out more than our share of writers persists, both within the state and without. I have heard it said that there is something in the water, but I grew up in the country on well water so sulfuric and metallic-tasting that, if it contained any magic literary potion, it was lost on me, because about all I did with it was spit it in the sink after brushing my teeth.

Fred Chappell, asked years ago about the high number of writers in the region in general, wrote that there is something chthonic in the soil itself. (I count on Fred to teach me words like chthonic; I only wish he would teach me how to pronounce them.) I confess to loving this notion of something underfoot that affords ordinary failures like myself some modest success at chronicling the lives of ordinary failures like myself. The county I grew up in produces more crops than any other in a state that ranks in the top ten for agricultural production in the Union. I like to think that this fertility extends to language. Sentences snaking up like shoots in the sandy soil.

I was born in the piedmont but my memories of its red clay and furniture factories are dim since we moved east when I was six. I lived in Clinton until I went to college in Boone. I can claim that I know the state fairly well, having lived—if I count only those towns where I spent more than a year—in Siler City, Clinton, Boone, Chapel Hill, Elizabeth City, Raleigh, and Greensboro. Briefly did I hover in Black Mountain, Laurinburg, and Wilmington. And I grew up visiting relatives in St. Paul's, Murfreesboro, Tarboro, and Montreat.

I spent some time in Seattle and three years in Charlottesville, Virginia, and I am writing this in Texas, where I now live part of the year, but wherever I go, I am purebred Tar Heel. My father is from Tarboro; my mother is from Lenoir. East meets west, and it happened in the middle of the state, in Chapel Hill. My mother was in graduate school studying history and my father was there on the G.I. Bill. Though she has traveled widely and is one of the least provincial people I know, my mother has lived in North Carolina her entire life. My father left only for a few months to work in the shipyards of Norfolk in the early '40s and, when the war broke out, spent a year on domestic army bases in Oregon and Texas and two years in the European theater. My father's side of the family has lived in the state as far back as we can trace. My maternal grandmother, the outlier in the bunch, came east from Lone Wolf, Oklahoma. (I don't mind that she's the only nonnative in the tree, because it sounds exotic for me to say I'm kin to anyone out of Lone Wolf, Oklahoma.) The man she married was—it shames me to admit—born in South Carolina, though my grandfather's family quickly came to their senses and moved across the border to Gastonia.

Of my eight books, 85 percent of the material is set in eastern North Carolina. My latest novel, *All I Have in This World*, is set here in Texas. Though the novel contains brief scenes in

Indiana, Ohio, Oregon, and coastal North Carolina, 90 percent of the action takes place in the high desert and ranch land of far West Texas. I was living there when I wrote the book. The landscape struck me immediately as about as foreign from where I usually set my stories as is possible. I would look out the window of the little adobe I was renting and see for miles—high flat desert broken only by the mountains bordering Mexico seventy miles distant. I wrote at 5,000 feet above sea level instead of a couple hundred. The earth was rocky and dusty, the only vegetation various kinds of cacti and creosote and, alongside the rare seasonal creek, a tough stand of cottonwood. Even though I lived for two decades in Greensboro (which the critic Lewis Mumford described, as far back as 1938, as "The Parking Lot City"), I have never set so much as a scene there. My little postage stamp of soil is the soggy coastal plain of my youth, disarmingly green and sunken, muggy, mostly windless, dimpled with lake, pond, and swamp, and, if you keep driving east for an hour, an ocean.

One of the central characters in *All I Have in This World* is a woman in her midfifties, a native West Texan, the child of a ranch hand and a stolid ranch hand's wife. Because she doesn't say a whole lot, she was a difficult character to write. In the first draft of the novel I was crazy proud of how I had nailed my laconic West Texan woman, but after the third of fourth draft I realized that what she *does* say, she says in the rhythms of eastern North Carolina.

No surprise that I could not even hear, for at least a year, how I had inflected her dialogue with the music of home. The wonderful and woefully underrated novelist and story writer William Goyen wrote in the preface of his *Collected Stories* of what his own birthplace had given him:

> I've cared about the buried song in somebody and sought
> it passionately: or the music in what happened. And
> so I have thought of my stories as folk song, as ballad,
> or rhapsody. This led me to be concerned with speech,

lyric speech—my heritage. Since the people of the region where most of my stories start—or end (they do, I believe, move in and through the great world)— are natural talkers and use their speech with gusto and often with the air and bravura of singers; and since the language of their place is rich with phrases and expressions of the King James Bible, from the Negro imagination and the Mexican fantasy, from Deep South Evangelism, from cotton field and cotton gin, oil field, railroad and sawmill, I had at my ears a glorious sound. A marvelous instrument of language was given to me.

I spent my teenaged years, as many of us did, wanting the hell out of the tiny, backwards, narrow-minded town where I lived. I always wanted to write fiction, but I did not think it was even remotely possible for me, because real life was passing by me daily, carried on elsewhere: Chapel Hill, New England, Greenwich Village, Haight-Ashbury. So—because I did not think it possible to come from such an unenlightened and barely literate place and become a serious writer—I indulged in the pastimes common to those of us who came of age in the early seventies: I leaned against Camaros or Mustangs or Monte Carlos in the parking lot of Hardee's listening to eight-tracks of *Exile on Main Street* and *Houses of the Holy* while under the influence of various substances. I kept myself numb, and I considered this numbness necessary to endure the tedium of my home.

When I began to write, seriously write at UNC—after a couple of failed attempts at other colleges—under the tutelage of such generous and encouraging writers as Lee Smith, Marianne Gingher, Daphne Athas, and Max Steele, it turned out that I was not so benumbed after all. Or, rather, I was neither as deaf nor as dumb as I thought. Though my first fledgling (and embarrassing) attempts at storytelling were heavily influenced by the inflectionless voices of the dominant writers of the '80s—the minimalists then in full publishing sway—in time I began to discover what Goyen referred to as "that glorious sound." And here is what my home has given me: a marvelous instrument of language so closely connected with landscape that I came to bless daily the happy accident of my birthplace.

Though a few of my fellow North Carolina writers favor a prose style one might describe as stripped-down or stark, most of us, no matter what geographical region of the state we come from, tend toward a more lyrical, if not downright maximalist, style. If a sentence is designed to become the very thing it describes (and if it is not, the hell with it), describing a late afternoon down-east thunderstorm in short, declarative sentences is not likely to encourage the reader to take cover. There is something about my watery part of the state that demands, to my mind, a syntax that resembles a map of the region. I can glance at that map and hear—at the sight of spindly roads broken by lake, bog, pocosin, sound—the idiom of home. If you can't get there from here—if the bridge is twenty miles north, if no one bothered to drain the swamp so they could put a road through it—it's no wonder that your prose is occasionally described as orbicular, if not convoluted. My prose is often riddled with asides (which, if you have read this far, I needn't point out to you) not because my characters are given to rarefied emotional or intellectual leaps, as in the work of Henry James, or because I am trying to emphasize the presence of the past in the present, as suggested by the parenthetical torrents of Faulkner, but because my sentences attempt to mimic their attempts to get to work on time in a terrain given to detour, if not dead end.

In an essay I wrote twenty years ago about the influence of Clinton on my work (a bit prematurely, since I had just published my first novel), I pinpointed an actual place which, then and now, seems the epicenter of whatever chthonic force supplied me with stories: an alleyway behind the office of the first newspaper my father owned in Clinton. I hung out there after school, waiting for a ride to our house two miles outside of town. It was in this alley that I first heard the low slow sensual soul music of the mid-to-late sixties. It spilled out of the black-owned barber shop and pool room sharing the alley, and seeped from the lips of the patrons, who drifted out into the alleyways also to do the things people do in alleyways the world over. The Chi-Lites, the Delfonics, the Impressions. Minnie Riperton, Eddie Holman, King Floyd, Al Green. When people ask me about my most important literary influences, I always say Flaubert, because I feel no one would take me seriously if I told the truth. If I could write one sentence — one — as moving as the way in which Otis Redding sings the lines "Plea-ee-ee-ease, let me sit down bes-i-i-i-ide you / I've got something to tell you you should know-o-o-o, whoa-o-o-o . . ." in the song "I Love You More Than Words Can Say," I might give all this up and get a job doing the only other thing I know how to do, which is accidentally messing up people's electronic devices.

A few years ago, when my siblings and I were midway through our yearly vacation at Emerald Isle, having dispensed with the traditional half pound of shrimp per person, sitting around the table eating ice cream, my father said, out of the blue, "I was in Frank's Hot Dogs one day when a man came up from Wilmington carrying a bag of snakes." One of my brothers or sisters said, under breath, but loud enough for all of us to hear, "*All* of your stories start that way." I can't say I'm used to people coming up from Wilmington with a bag of snakes, but I'm so used to stories that start in such a manner that I hardly recognize the oddity of it. Flannery O'Connor, in her essay "Some Aspects of the Grotesque in Southern Fiction," said, "Whenever I'm asked why Southern writers particularly have a penchant for writing about freaks, I say it is because we are still able to recognize one." I might be able to recognize one in person, especially if he came into a hot dog joint carrying a bag of snakes, but when described to me in conversation by a friend or relative from home, I don't spot the novelty in it.

MICHAEL PARKER

William Goyen described the people he grew up with as "natural talkers." I am resistant to regional literary stereotypes when they are applied to any region, but I am particularly prickly about them when they are directed toward the work of me and my fellow North Carolinians, not only because they are clueless, but because they are often antediluvian. When writers like Richard Price or David Simon locate the poetry in everyday speech, they are praised by critics for their finely tuned ear for vernacular, but when someone from south of D.C. and east of Ohio does the same, reviewers trot out pejorative and outdated terms like "dialect" and "local color."

And yet I will concede that my relatives are perhaps more inclined to tell you a long-ass story than people from elsewhere. Around our dinner table, a story can take forever to tell because there are always interruptions. Many of these are inquiries that people from other parts of the country might find maddeningly irrelevant (what does he do, who did he marry, where did he go to school?). A story, weighed down with endless dashes and parentheses, begins to resemble a map of those got-to-go-around-your-ass-to-get-to-your-elbow roads.

I do not know why the man came up from Wilmington carrying a bag of snakes. I do not know what happened when he walked into Frank's Place. As soon as my father uttered the words "Frank's Place," I remembered that the hot dog stand shared the alley with the black pool room and barber shop, and I heard, in my father's opening line, that sweet, slow, soulful music of home. ("Plea—ee-ee-ease let me sit down beside you / I got something to tell you you should know-o-o-o-whoa!") Like William Goyen, I am less interested in what actually happened than in its music, and so I won't be asking my father to repeat a tale that I was too preoccupied to listen to the first time around. He'd never tell it the same way, anyway.

Writing by Ear

JILL MCCORKLE

In his poem "At the Wellhead," the poet Seamus Heaney wrote: *Your songs, when you sing them with your two eyes closed as you always do, are like a local road we've known every turn of in the past.* I felt drawn to those lines from first reading, picturing not roads in Ireland where I have never been, or the Massachusetts roads I was driving and seeing daily at the time, but roads in my native North Carolina, familiar roads that it seemed I had always known—some still there and others not. The poem continues, leading to my favorite line: *sing yourself to where the singing comes from.* I think this line serves as an accurate description of the writing life, and all those times we return to those earliest sights and sounds that shaped our lives, a process so rhythmic and familiar we often can only see it with the distance of years or miles.

The childhood years of my children were very different from my own. I grew up in Lumberton, North Carolina, always praying for snow but instead knowing hot humid summers and Christmas mornings so mild that all the bikes and skates and balls that Santa had left behind filled the neighborhood streets as the sun was rising. My childhood family vacations were trips to the beach—an hour-plus drive along Highway 211 through the Green Swamp. I once complained to my Dad that I had nothing educational to report on the first day of school, a statement I came to regret since after that he always suggested we go to Fort Fisher. I had all the information on Fort Fisher that any one person needed to have, and was finally relieved when we ventured out of the state to visit relatives first in Marietta, Georgia, and then in Annapolis, Maryland. However, those trips, though fun, could not really compete with days spent at the beach; by then, my whole life was measured by memories and collected shells from the previous trip and anticipations of the next.

My children grew up over six hundred miles northward, just outside of Boston. They knew winters when two feet of snow was not unusual, and their summers often included visits to a lake in New Hampshire—water so cold that their lips and fingers were often blue. My elementary school field trips had been to Dainty Mae's bakery in downtown Lumberton, where we got to suck icing out of a pastry bag, and then to the fire department, where (if you behaved) you were allowed to slide down the fire pole. My children visited Paul Revere's house and biked to Walden Pond. They took a class trip to the Cape. But they also visited North Carolina often through those years, and they shared my love for the much warmer waters of the Carolina coast as well as for grits and country ham. For a long period in their young lives, they even thought it would be exciting to slide down a fire pole, suck icing from the pastry bag, and possibly visit Fort Fisher.

My son came home from kindergarten one day furious at a classmate. When I finally got him to tell me what all the fuss was about, I learned that the boy in question had told Rob that I have an accent. I quickly responded: *Well, I do*, at which point his eyes got wide in surprise and he said, *I never knew that*. Afterwards, it seemed there was at times a study of my words—the difference in pen and pin and such. My daughter could imitate "southern" and did so often; I once overheard her telling a group of friends "I'm suthin like my mutha" to a chorus of giggles. There was one child in their elementary school who liked to come over and follow me around. I was told he liked to hear me talk, and when with me, he'd sometimes repeat words, echoing what I had said. When he saw that I heard him, he would break into an overexaggerated mimicry that left everyone laughing until a later time when he would privately return to his earnest shaping of sounds. I learned several years later that he had been adopted and that, in fact, he had been born in North Carolina.

This was not the first time I had wondered about a human's first memories of sound—especially those that might predate birth. The notion of voice and the origin of our voices is exactly where I am headed with this idea. As a writer, my voice has always remained tied to my North Carolina source even though I spent twenty years living and raising children elsewhere. I, too, would have first heard southern voices as an infant, and it would have been rare for an accent to have entered my pre-birthing that did not match the accents I grew up with. As a writer, I realize that I am often inspired and driven by auditory triggers.

We all know the power of music and the way we sometimes respond to a song, the sounds tugging us back into another place and bringing along other senses that help to form a whole picture of the past. I'm often searching my mind for the voices of those people now lost to life. Oddly, I sometimes find that they are more real and closer to truth in my mind than what I might hear on some old antiquated cassette tape. I wrote one novel in particular with no other destination than to catch and preserve the voices of my grandmother and great-aunt. My aunt died during the writing. My grandmother touched the cover, but her reach was out of dementia and near the very end of her life. Still, the sound of their voices continued to pull, sometimes urging me to attempt to phonetically write them down, the lilts and pitches, the little chuckle that accompanied things my grandmother felt were ugly and should NOT be laughed at and yet she did, or the slight snore, almost like the puttering of a distant dying motorboat, as I lay there in her featherbed, a five-year-old, excited to spend the night and spend a day in her world—so different from my own. I fell asleep to cars passing on the street in front of her house, a street that had become very busy in recent years, not at all the way it was when my parents were growing up—my mother in that very house, and my dad just a few blocks away. The car lights would circle the room and the sound of engines close and then far, pulled me to sleep until my grandmother rose in early morning darkness.

Time with my grandmother was like being in a time machine and venturing back to a time when the day was defined by sunrise and sunset and physical labor—tending her garden, a quarter-acre lot that she grew every summer, putting away enough vegetables to keep us all (and lucky friends) in corn and field peas and okra and tomatoes the whole year through. Her neighborhood in late summer was filled with the rumble of tobacco trucks heading to the nearby warehouses, that whole part of town blanketed in the heavy sweet smell I love to this day. In my mind, that whole scene remains vivid, and I find that I often have to drive by to recall that it is vastly different now, that my grandmother's white house with the front porch with swing and glider has not been there for years. There has been a market and a Laundromat and now a storefront church that looks to have shut down as well.

A couple of years ago, I took my mother and her cousin (who had grown up just down the block) for a ride. Both of them suffer from dementia and almost nothing remains of the world they knew as children, and yet they asked me repeatedly to drive back by. "I know it's here somewhere," my mother's cousin said, her forehead pressed to the window, eyes hopeful. "It's close. I know we're very close."

Sometimes when I drive to the coast, I am struck by how very little the road there has changed. It's swampland and so nothing can be built and there are still pockets through the Green Swamp where you can't get a phone signal. There is silence on that stretch of road. At one end of my journey is the interstate stretching along the East Coast, and at the other is the Atlantic Ocean. My characters travel this road often, perhaps because I also travel it—physically and mentally—as a touchstone that pulls me back to the source of not only my fiction but my life.

I think voice is one of the most powerful resources a writer has, and for me the early background music of life, the constant beat that like a steady pulse seemed to hold everything together, was the sound of the ocean and then the sound of trucks out on Interstate 95 (which to me sounded *like* the ocean; I often fell asleep pretending that it was).

The ocean and the interstate are always present in my work. They pull my characters in one way or another. I had an immediate love for Boston, and I think it's because I still had the Atlantic Ocean within a short drive and still lived close enough to I-95 that I heard the familiar and constant whoosh of tires on pavement, a sound that late at night is not unlike what I heard when my children were in the womb and viewed with ultrasound. The swish and lull of amniotic fluid, the steady rhythmic beat of a heart.

My daughter was born in Boston, two weeks late, during one of the hottest Julys on record. I spent much of my time in that last month going to the video store and loading up on rentals that I would watch in a dark room cooled by one rumbling window unit. I had watched a lot of Hitchcock and done things like an Audrey Hepburn marathon, but then I began thinking of movies I hadn't seen in years, not since seated in the cool of the Carolina Theatre in Lumberton with my sister and cousin and best friend. We could go to the theatre and stay all day, see the one o'clock show and then the three. They didn't clear the theatre. We could just go and set up camp, which we often did, armed with popcorn and Charms suckers and those big dill pickles they sold in bags. Sometimes we watched the movie and sometimes we just whispered and laughed there in the cool darkness until someone of authority came to reprimand us. I remember watching *Gone with the Wind* post intermission—well into the carpetbagging years—when my cousin leaned close to me and said, "Who is Tara? The baby?" We have laughed for years over that one.

Our movie choices had plots that were usually pretty easy

to follow, and trips to the candy counter or bathroom didn't interrupt the flow. Jerry Lewis and Dean Martin movies. Elvis Presley or Annette Funicello/Frankie Avalon movies. We saw them all. But of course our favorites were the Disneys, and more than the animated Disneys, the ones with Hayley Mills and Dean Jones and Kurt Russell and Fred MacMurray. *The Parent Trap* and *That Darn Cat!* and *The Absent-Minded Professor* and *Flubber*. And mixed in there with all the others was my very favorite: *The Three Lives of Thomasina*. It was made when I was five, so my first viewing of it would have been that year or soon after.

These were the movies I was renting to carry me to my daughter's birth. This video store had a whole section of oldies, and so it was the first time since childhood that I had gotten to see these favorites. I marveled at how differently I had remembered it all. Some stood the test of time. Others seemed silly and contrived, and yet, I lay there like a beached whale, my daughter shifting from side to side, as I watched.

How had I never noticed that *Thomasina* took place in Scotland? And that in fact the characters *all* had accents? I had spent years of my life wanting to be the beautiful witch in the woods who sings and weaves and heals and takes in animals of all kinds. And how had I forgotten that the cat herself narrates? And yet, the sound of her voice, telling her tale, had an incredible power in that cool darkened room, while the blazing glare of July blanketed the outside world. Thomasina had three very distinct lives, finally finding her way back home to her original owner.

Several years later, when my daughter was not yet four—videos still rented at the likes of Blockbuster and many old movies still not easily found—I once again stumbled on *Thomasina* and excitedly rented it and told her that we were going to watch a movie I had loved when I was just a little bit older than she was. I told her the name and she immediately said: "Is this the one about the cat?" And then in child language with lots of animated hand movement she gave her

JILL MCCORKLE

200

version of *Thomasina*. When I questioned her, she said she watched it back when she was inside of me; she said that there was a TV in there.

I was speechless and remain so when I think of it. I'm sure that there might be many different hypotheses for how this might have happened, but I suspect that I will never be fully convinced of anything other than just what she said. She listened to the sounds of those voices in the womb, as I was there listening in what was my own kind of simulated womb and allowing myself to pretend that I was in the cool darkness of the Carolina Theatre—Lumberton, North Carolina, 1963.

The sound of that movie was familiar to her, as was my southern accent, as were the many different and varying Massachusetts accents she encountered. I was already a believer in how we are tethered to our sources in ways that are often surprising, often so subtle we don't even see the connecting filaments until years later when the spark occurs and we are pulled back into what is familiar. I also was born in the heat of July and would have entered a world of oscillating fans and garden sprinklers, the creak of gliders and the hum of hymns and cars passing down the very road that leads to the coast. The source of my voice—where the singing comes from—and the voices that guide my writing life are older than I am—the umbilical cord forever unwinding and yet tethered to and dependent on the constant pulse of a place called home.

Water Everywhere

BLAND SIMPSON

When Hurricane Hazel's powerhouse sidewinds and torrential rains swiped northeastern North Carolina the day before my sixth birthday, October 15th, 1954, water piled up and lay everywhere in Elizabeth City. Water filled the side ditches and ran the creeks out of their banks, and the long, thin, drooping branches of the willow trees caressed the flooding streets and yards. Less than a year later, when Hurricanes Connie, Diane, and Ione roared through the sound country in quick, late-summer succession, dropping nearly fifty inches of rain, water again stood everywhere, and the bay-like Pasquotank River spread out, and for a spell our homes seemed to be in the very river itself.

Though the hurricane rises were acknowledged extra, water everywhere was what we always knew, and expected. Three of the four property lines around my family's West Williams Circle home were ditches, cut to drain a huge cornfield out back, so that modest postwar houses could be built along the outer edge of a turn-of-the-twentieth-century horse-racing track. Less than two blocks away was Gaither's Lagoon, a dense, jungled, swampy backwater off the Pasquotank, which itself was only two blocks farther on. Eighteen miles south was the vast Albemarle Sound, known in early colonial days as the Sea of Roanoke, an inland ocean to English eyes. Eighteen miles north was the vast morass of the Great Dismal Swamp.

A drive east of little over an hour got us to the Atlantic Ocean, though as a gull flies the sea was scarcely thirty miles away. The cold, blue Atlantic at Nags Head, blue crabs in a basket in the kitchen of my grandmother's cottage, these were among my earliest memories. So was a fried-chicken picnic, with ginger ales in a Scotch-plaid cylindrical cooler, down at Texaco Beach on the lower Pasquotank River, halfway from Elizabeth City to the Albemarle Sound.

A drive west of just a few minutes propelled us over the Perquimans River's S-curve bridge—upon which the old crooning tune *Carolina Moon* was written—and not long thereafter over the broad, three-mile-wide Chowan, then over the tiny Cashie, and then across Conine Creek, Conine Island (another jungle, the miles-wide Roanoke bottom), and over the muscly, brown-water Roanoke River.

North, beyond the Great Dismal, my cousins in Virginia Beach lived high up a dune on 61st Street overlooking the Atlantic, behind that dune a forest filled with shallow, sparkling freshwater ponds. Then the cousins moved to Little Creek Navy Base, right on a branch, where we fished for carp with dough balls, and, after that, on to Bayside, a half a mile from Chesapeake Bay. There we young boys swam and walked and sailed a catamaran by day and sat out on the anchored craft by night, telling jokes and speculating on romance and how it all worked, admiring the phosphorescent trails our hands and arms made as we moved them in the mysterious waters.

We must have thought of ourselves as amphibians—we certainly *acted* like amphibians, given what all we did and where all we did it. These many waters—swamps, ponds, creeks, canals, branches of the bay—were as much a part of our daily lives as our daily bread. They were everywhere we went and they told us how to get where we were going, which turns to make in order to get to a narrow place, a log or plank across a stream, a bridge over something bigger, and so forth, and where roads were and could even begin *to be* in such low, wet country.

The Navy flew blimps from its base on the Pasquotank River, and the Coast Guard flew float planes from its enclave nearby. Fishing boats came up the river from down on the sound, holds full of fish, and the Globe Fish Company on

Water Street was ready for them, ready to box and ice and ship their wares to Norfolk, Baltimore, New York. When President Franklin Delano Roosevelt trained down from Washington to Elizabeth City in August 1937, on his way to attend Paul Green's drama *The Lost Colony* on Roanoke Island on the 350th anniversary of the birth of Virginia Dare, what did he do? He went by water: he boarded a Coast Guard vessel at Water Street, cruised down the Pasquotank River, with Coast Guardsman Louis Midgette pointing out the sights, crossed the broad Albemarle, and sailed right on into Shallowbag Bay to a tumbledown fuel dock in Manteo.

And then he went to the Waterside Theatre and took in the show.

All family tales were set upon eastern waters, or mentioned them in passing—not to do so was impossible. Yet we left the waters behind once, I thought. That was when we moved to Chapel Hill in 1959, to the middle of the landlocked province of the piedmont upstate. Or did we? A beautiful unnamed creek flowed through a sycamore forest, the narrow valley of Battle Park, the woods that lay between my grandparents' home on Franklin Street and my aunt and uncle's home at the bottom of the big Raleigh Road hill. That creek and forest and hill soon stood in for my left-behind Gaither's Lagoon.

In Chapel Hill, we Boy Scouts met in a cabin at Eastwood Lake (also once known as Grandma's Lake, where a furious, murderous Duke student had once disposed of his grandmother, who according to legend refused him money, by pitching her into that big pond). When the troop took off for the mountains, where I first saw the astonishing high blue hills of western Caroline, Wolfe's Old Catawba, we were also going to a lake, to Fontana, the fountain, for a sixty-mile canoe trek from Bryson City on the eastern end of the great impoundment to its western end, where the big curved dam was, and back. A little pine slab footstool I paid $8.00 for in Cherokee so I'd have a souvenir to bring my mother, and which she quickly, tacitly, gave back to me (it seemed to suit my room more than hers, she mused), still serves as a keen reminder of that week in the jump-up country and on the big waters of Fontana.

If one is lucky, one may well be drawn often to the object of one's affection. Mine, clearly, has been water, mostly that of our coast and coastal plain, and the people who love it, and love floating on it, fishing in it, studying its birds and plants, for whatever reason simply seeking it out. My wife, Ann, grew up in Sea Level, North Carolina, watching shrimp boats from her bedroom window, seeing their lights at night and listening to their low-thrumming, diesel-engine sounds as they worked the waters of Nelson's Bay just off Core Sound. My Sea Level sweetheart and I long ago lost count of how many returns, revisits, explorations, and launches we have made back into the water-loving lands that formed us.

From *captivated* to *captured* by my watery ancestral lands has turned out to be a lucky short march indeed. First, the vaunted *Chapel Hill Weekly* editor Jim Shumaker (later a crusty, beloved UNC School of Journalism professor and archetypal progenitor of protégé Jeff MacNelly's comic strip *Shoe*) told me he would publish an essay of mine about John Foley's and my September 1972 trip into the Great Dismal Swamp, which he did. Second, over the next two years, Loyd Little and Jerry Adams of the *Carolina Financial Times* assigned me to go write a number of features relating to eastern North Carolina: profile the smallest bank in the state in Macclesfield; tell about scuppernong growing; look at zoning, or the lack of it, on the Outer Banks. A decade and a half later, I went back into the Great Dismal in earnest, married my Sea Level sweetheart, and then set off with her into the whole chain of sound-country swamps, poquosons, rivers great and small, and into as much of the wide, wild estuarine world as we could get our arms around.

My parents had reared me in a home close to where a small swamp stream became a big river. The big river turned out to be connected to the Albemarle Lagoon, the largest enclosed embayment in the world, the inland sea that the earliest Euro-peans mistook for the Pacific Ocean. Our many waters are so vast, their magnetism, their spell, their power is so sublime: the long views the sounds afford, the long, light waves when the wind is at peace, the sunsets over the sounds and those way up the long rivers Pamlico and Neuse and Roanoke that flow into the sounds from the west, the thousands of miles of vacant estuarine shores, the marshes, the drowned woodlands and intertwined tree-trunk boneyards. Skiffs, scows, dugouts, canoes, mothboats, ferry flats, *ghost schooners*—they all sailed through stories my father told me, others that my grandfather spun, recalling schooners laid up at the Tar Landing and the New River wharf, ready to receive barrels of rosin from the Onslow turpentine orchards and sail away. They sailed through tales told and read at school, through songs sung in waterfront shebangs and on stages up and down the coast.

They even sailed through my dreams, and still do.

One of those dreams, by far the greatest, is about vigor-ously protecting these enormously productive estuarine wa-ters, as well as restoring their health wherever they are im-paired. The dream is not one I made up, but really a gift that I received. As a young attorney, my father worked to create a better, healthier water system for Elizabeth City, one that would stop the town's fouling of the Pasquotank River, upon whose banks our town, nicknamed "Queen of the Albemarle," had been built. Always remembering his efforts, his deep be-liefs about stewardship of our natural resources, I have tried to help bring such faith and works forward into my own time, for this much is clear and irrefutable: *the health of the water is the same as the health of the people.* Inasmuch as we protect and restore the vast estuarine waters for ourselves and our children and our progeny, we also demonstrate *that* it can be done and *how* it can be done, and we do so with this invita-tion, also an invocation: *let us make our many waters living models to the world.*

So, for this river-port-town boy, how could it all not have

been about water, about our many waters? A hungry eye, they say, can see a long way, and in any landscape near or far, my eyes have always fed restlessly for water. Where was it? Where was the draw, the divide, the run, the rill, the prong, or the branch one might follow down to the point where it collected, with other such runs, and then flowed slowly, broadened, became a river, and got a name?

In the time before names, the ancient land-bridge pilgrims walking east found our wet, jungled, water-everywhere territory millennia ago, millennia before anyone from Spain or England sailed west to get here, a long time before there were any such countries from which to set sail. Perhaps the souls of so many untold generations of strivers in this place float free out over the rivers and sounds on the long sunset light, or hang in the mists after sound-country rains—if one believes in ghosts, perhaps so. Something makes us stand at the shallows of rivers, sounds, oceans, and stare, something pulls us into a stance of vigil, as if in the air and light upon the clouds, answers and calls either voiced or set in ciphers or printed as signs and symbols may yet appear. Who would wish to miss them? Are we not pulled, ebbed and flowed, by the moon as much as any of these waters and their tides?

If the answers are not on the waves, in the winds that drive them, in the clouds that rise above them, where on earth, pray, could they possibly be at all?

Contributors

ROSECRANS BALDWIN is the author of *Paris, I Love You but You're Bringing Me Down* and *You Lost Me There*. He frequently reviews books on NPR and has taught creative writing at UNC–Chapel Hill.

WILL BLYTHE is editor at large for Byliner.com and the author of *To Hate Like This Is To Be Happy Forever*. A former literary editor of *Esquire*, he's a frequent contributor to the *New York Times Book Review* as well as the *New Yorker*, *Rolling Stone*, and *Sports Illustrated*. His work has been anthologized in *The Best American Short Stories* and *The Best American Sportswriting*. Raised in Chapel Hill, North Carolina, Blythe now lives and works in New York City.

BELLE BOGGS's first book, *Mattaponi Queen*, is a collection of linked stories published by Graywolf Press. *Mattaponi Queen* won the Bakeless Prize and the Library of Virginia Award, was short-listed for the 2010 Frank O'Connor Short Story Award, was long-listed for the Story Prize, and was a finalist for the Library of Virginia People's Choice Award for fiction. Her next two books, *The Art of Waiting*, a collection of essays, and *The Ugly Bear List*, a novel, will also be published by Graywolf. Her fiction and nonfiction have appeared in the *Paris Review*, *Orion*, *Harper's*, *Slate*, *Salon*, the *Sun*, and the *Oxford American*, among other publications. She lives in Chatham County, North Carolina, with her husband, daughter, and two cats.

FRED CHAPPELL, who was born in Canton, taught for forty years at UNC–Greensboro. From 1997 to 2002 he served as the Poet Laureate of North Carolina. He has produced over thirty volumes of fiction, poetry, and nonfiction and is perhaps best known for his tetralogy of novels centering on the life and times of Jess Kirkman, a fictional denizen of western North Carolina. Chappell's latest volume of poems, *Familiars*, was published in 2014 by Louisiana State University Press. Other work slated for publication includes a *Masters of the Weird Tale* volume and what he mysteriously refers to only as "the Shadow novel." Chappell confesses that, since retirement, he "writes, reads, talks incessantly, and nourishes vague hopes," and that his wife, Susan Nicholls Chappell, "protects him from himself—with spotty success."

JAN DEBLIEU is the author of four books about natural history and sense of place and the winner of the national John Burroughs Medal for Natural History Writing. For the past five years, she has been exploring how one might live a life of true service to others. Her forthcoming book will detail that journey. She lives on Roanoke Island.

PAMELA DUNCAN was born in Asheville and raised in Black Mountain, Swannanoa, and Shelby, North Carolina. She currently lives in Cullowhee, where she teaches creative writing at Western Carolina University. She is the author of three novels—*Moon Women*, *Plant Life*, and *The Big Beautiful*. She is at work on *The Wilder Place*, a novel set in western North Carolina, and a collection of short stories. Visit her website at www.pameladuncan.com.

CLYDE EDGERTON is the author of ten novels, including *Walking across Egypt* and *The Night Train*, and two books of nonfiction. His latest book is *Papadaddy's Book for New Fathers*, illustrated by Daniel Wallace. He is a member of the Fellowship of Southern Writers and is the Thomas S. Kenan III Distinguished Professor of Creative Writing at UNC–Wilmington.

BEN FOUNTAIN was born in Chapel Hill and grew up in the tobacco country of eastern North Carolina. He is the author of a story collection, *Brief Encounters with Che Guevara*, and a novel, *Billy Lynn's Long Halftime Walk*. His work has received the PEN/Hemingway Award, the National Book Critics' Circle Award for Fiction, and the Los Angeles Times Book Prize for Fiction and has been a finalist for the National Book Award. He has lived in Texas since 1983.

MARIANNE GINGHER's books include the novel *Bobby Rex's Greatest Hit*, which was made into an NBC movie, and two memoirs, *A Girl's Life: Horses, Boys, Weddings, and Luck* and *Adventures in Pen Land*. Most recently she edited an anthology of flash fiction by sixty-five North Carolina writers, *Long Story Short*, published by UNC Press. Her nonfiction has also appeared in the *Oxford American*, the *New York Times*, the *Washington Post Magazine*, *Veranda*, *O, The Oprah Magazine*, and *Our State*. Currently a Bowman and Gordon Gray Distinguished Term Professor, she teaches creative writing at UNC–Chapel Hill. In 2009 she and collaborator Deborah Seabrooke founded Jabberbox Puppet Theater, specializing in comedic puppetry for adults.

JUDY GOLDMAN's memoir, *Losing My Sister*, was a finalist for Southeast Booksellers Alliance's and *ForeWord Review*'s Memoir of the Year, and an excerpt appeared in *Real Simple* magazine. She is also the author of two novels, *Early Leaving* and *The Slow Way Back*, as well as two books of poetry. Her work has won the Sir Walter Raleigh Fiction Award, the Mary Ruffin Poole First Fiction Award, the Gerald Cable Poetry Prize, and the top three prizes for poetry in North Carolina. She's been published in the *Southern Review*, the *Gettysburg Review*, the *Kenyon Review*, the *Ohio Review*, *Prairie Schooner*, *Shenandoah*, and the *Washington Post*. She and her husband have two married children and four grandchildren.

STEPHANIE ELIZONDO GRIEST is a globe-trotting author and activist from South Texas. Her books include the memoirs *Around the Bloc: My Life in Moscow, Beijing, and Havana* and *Mexican Enough: My Life between the Borderlines*, as well as the best-selling guidebook *100 Places Every Woman Should Go*. She has also written for the *New York Times*, the *Washington Post*, the *Believer*, the *Oxford American*, the *Wilson Quarterly*, *Latina*, and *Earth Island Journal*, and she edited *Best Women's Travel Writing 2010*. In 2013 she became assistant professor of creative nonfiction at the University of North Carolina at Chapel Hill. Visit her website at Stephanie ElizondoGriest.com.

RANDALL KENAN is the author of a novel, *A Visitation of Spirits*; two works of nonfiction, *Walking on Water: Black American Lives at the Turn of the Twenty-First Century* and *The Fire This Time*; and a collection of stories, *Let the Dead Bury Their Dead*. He edited and wrote the introduction for *The Cross of Redemption: The Uncollected Writings of James Baldwin*. Among his awards are a Guggenheim Fellowship, the North Carolina Award, and the American Academy of Arts and Letters Rome Prize. He is a professor of English and comparative literature at UNC–Chapel Hill.

JILL MCCORKLE's most recent novel, *Life After Life*, was published in 2013. She is the author of nine previous books—four story collections and five novels—five of which have been selected as *New York Times* Notable Books. The recipient of the New England Book Award, the John Dos Passos Prize for Excellence in Literature, and the North Carolina Prize for Literature, she has taught writing at Harvard, Brandeis, UNC–Chapel Hill, and N.C. State University. A native of Lumberton, she currently lives in Hillsborough, North Carolina.

MICHAEL MCFEE has published fourteen books, most recently a collection of poetry, *That Was Oasis*, a chapbook of one-line poems, *The Smallest Talk*, and a collection of prose, *The Napkin Manuscripts: Selected Essays and an Interview*. He has received the James Still Award for Writing about the Appalachian South from the Fellowship of Southern Writers, the Thomas Wolfe Literary Award from the Western North Carolina Historical Association, and the R. Hunt Parker Memorial Award for lifetime literary achievement from the North Carolina Literary and Historical Association. A native of Asheville, North Carolina, he has taught in the Creative Writing Program at UNC–Chapel Hill for several decades.

LYDIA MILLET is the author of eleven books of fiction, including *Magnificence* (2012), the last in a trilogy about extinction and loss, which was short-listed for the National Book Critics' Circle and *Los Angeles Times* book awards. Her story collection *Love in Infant Monkeys* was a finalist for the Pulitzer Prize, and a new novel, *Mermaids in Paradise*, came out from W. W. Norton in the fall of 2014.

ROBERT MORGAN is the author of fourteen books of poetry, including *Terroir* (2011), nine works of fiction, including *The Road from Gap Creek* (2013), and three volumes of nonfiction, including *Lions of the West* (2011). A new novel, *North Star*, will be published in 2015. A native of western North Carolina, he has taught at Cornell University since 1971.

JENNY OFFILL is the author of two novels, *Last Things* and *Dept. of Speculation*. She teaches in the low-residency writing program at Queens University in Charlotte, North Carolina.

MICHAEL PARKER is the author of six novels and two collections of stories, including his latest work, *All I Have in This World*, published in 2014. His fiction and nonfiction and essays have been published in the *New York Times*, the *New York Times Magazine*, the *Washington Post*, *Runner's World*, *Men's Journal*, and other publications. He has received awards and fellowships from the National Endowment for the Arts, the Pushcart Prize anthology, and the O. Henry Prize Stories and three career achievement awards: the North Carolina Award for Literature, the Hobson Award for Arts and Letters, and the R. Hunt Parker Award.

BLAND SIMPSON is Kenan Distinguished Professor of English and Creative Writing at the University of North Carolina at Chapel Hill, and he is a longtime member of the Tony Award–winning Red Clay Ramblers. He has collaborated on such musicals as *Diamond Studs, Kudzu, Fool Moon,* and *King Mackerel & the Blues Are Running.* His books include *The Great Dismal, Into the Sound Country* and *The Inner Islands* (both with photography by his wife, Ann Cary Simpson), and *The Coasts of Carolina* (with photography by Scott Taylor). In 2005 Simpson was given the North Carolina Award for Fine Arts, the state's highest civilian honor.

LEE SMITH is the author of sixteen works of fiction, including her latest novel, *Guests on Earth,* published in the fall of 2013. She has received many awards, including the North Carolina Award for Literature and an Academy Award in Fiction from the American Academy of Arts and Letters; her novel *The Last Girls* was a *New York Times* best seller as well as a winner of the Southern Book Critics Circle Award.

WELLS TOWER is the author of *Everything Ravaged, Everything Burned,* a collection of short stories. He grew up in Chapel Hill, North Carolina, and lives there still.

MONIQUE TRUONG was born in 1968 in South Vietnam and immigrated with her family to Boiling Springs, North Carolina. She is a novelist and essayist now based in Brooklyn, New York. Her first novel, *The Book of Salt,* was a national best seller, a *New York Times* Notable Fiction Book, and the recipient of the New York Public Library Young Lions Fiction Award, among other honors. Her second novel, *Bitter in the Mouth,* received the Rosenthal Family Foundation Award from the American Academy of Arts and Letters and was named a best fiction book of the year by Barnes & Noble and Hudson Booksellers. Her shorter works can be found in anthologies such as *A Fork in the Road* and *The Book of Men.*